THE GREATEST CATCHERS OF ALL TIME

THE GREATEST CATCHERS OF ALL TIME

First Edition

Donald Honig

 Wm. C. Brown Publishers

For My Daughter, Catherine

ACKNOWLEDGMENTS

For assistance in gathering the photographs used in this book, the author would like to express his appreciation to Patricia Kelly and her tireless colleagues at the National Baseball Hall of Fame and Museum at Cooperstown, New York; and to Michael P. Aronstein of TV Sports Mailbag.

Gratitude must also be expressed to Tom Heitz and Bill Deane, librarian and chief research assistant, respectively, of the National Baseball Hall of Fame and Museum, for sharing their vast knowledge of baseball history. The author is also appreciative of the astute consultation he received from the following: Stanley Honig, David Markson, Lawrence Ritter, Jeffrey Neuman, Ron Smith, and Bobby Bragan.

The Donald Honig
Best Players of All Time Series

By Donald Honig

Nonfiction

Fiction

Sidewalk Caesar
Walk Like a Man
Divide the Night
No Song to Sing
Judgment Night
The Love Thief
The Severith Style
Illusions
I Should Have Sold Petunias
The Last Great Season
Marching Home

CONTENTS

INTRODUCTION

The catcher is a ballplayer with few luxuries; he is also the one player whose most important contributions to his team's success go unnoticed by the public. In a game of speed and grace, he is encased in archaic-looking equipment and forced to spend most of his playing time in a squatting position. He is expected to take punishment, and he does. In a game in which crucial decisions are often based on inches and milliseconds and thus easily provokes frustration and ill temper, he is permitted neither, for it is incumbent on him more than any other player on the field to keep a clear balance of mind and disposition, for he is doing most of the thinking for the most pivotal man in the game—his teammate on the mound. His disagreements with the umpire—and they are more numerous than most fans realize—must be conducted quietly and discreetly, for he must coexist for nine innings with the man peering over his shoulder.

The catcher will call an average of 120 pitches in a game. None of them should be arbitrary. A good catcher will have purpose and logic behind every call, at the same time anticipating a batter's intent and maintaining the pitcher's confidence.

For other fielders there are the crowd-pleasing opportunities of running catches, dazzling stops, snappy pickups; for the catcher a defensive gem might be the gritty blocking of a pitch in the dirt, a most underappreciated effort, but one that can save a run and maybe a game. The catcher's most exciting defensive contribution, blocking a runner attempting to score, usually ends with him sprawled unglamorously on the ground with the crowd applauding the accuracy of the outfielder's throw.

But baseball people appreciate a good catcher and value him highly, which is why some catchers have long careers despite feeble batting averages. "He is the psychologist and historian" for the staff, wrote Jacques Barzun. The word "historian" is aptly chosen, for good catchers will remember what pitch a batter hit and under what circumstances, going back months, maybe years. The intelligent pitcher might also, but it is the man behind the plate who will be calling the pitch and fixing with his glove the spot to which it should be thrown.

Any list attempting to inscribe "the greatest" in a category leaves the selector vulnerable on all sides, particularly when the subject is baseball, a game that breeds adamant experts. Every man's angle of vision produces judgments that are valid. There may be a slight imprecision in the title of this book, for when the list of catchers to be included was being drawn up the emphasis was placed less on "all time" and more on the best of baseball's ever-changing eras. Thus some latter-day catchers with high batting averages and more impressive slugging records were omitted in favor of men from modern baseball's embryo years like Johnny Kling and Roger Bresnahan because they were then regarded as the game's top catchers. If a man was dominant in his time, he belongs in a compilation such as this, otherwise we run the danger of blurring historical perspective and nullifying all that has gone before.

THE GREATEST CATCHERS OF ALL TIME

Roger Bresnahan.

ROGER BRESNAHAN

Roger Bresnahan is remembered today primarily for having invented shin guards for catchers, and although it is always nice to be remembered for a positive contribution, Bresnahan's famous shin guards have come to obscure the fact that he was considered by many to be baseball's top catcher during the early years of the twentieth century. An indication of this esteem is his early election to the Hall of Fame in 1945, just nine years after baseball's Valhalla was opened; he was, in fact, the first twentieth century catcher to be installed at Cooperstown.

Bresnahan's nickname was "The Duke of Tralee," Tralee being the town in Ireland where for years he had people believing he had been born. This was a bit of Bresnahan blarney, for he had been born an ocean and a half continent away, in Toledo, Ohio, on June 11, 1879. The whimsical Irishman, who started his professional career as a pitcher, told gullible writers that he became a pitcher by learning to put a curve on the potatoes he tossed around Tralee.

Bresnahan's first whiff of big league glory came in 1897 as an eighteen-year-old pitcher with the Washington club of the National League (then the only major league). The youngster had a 4–0 record for his work at the end of the season, but when he and the club had a difference of opinion over what salary he should earn the next year, he was released.

After several years during which he played semipro ball, with a few, brief forays in and out of the professional ranks, Bresnahan showed up in a Chicago Cubs uniform at the end of the 1900 season, getting into one game. By then he was a catcher.

"Roger had a catcher's personality," said Fred Lieb, the longtime baseball writer who knew Bresnahan in the early years of the century. "Not only did he have to be out there every day, but he had very strong leadership instincts. He enjoyed the responsibilities that a catcher has; in fact, I think he thrived on them."

When the American League was formed in 1901, Bresnahan jumped to its Baltimore club. A year later, along

● *Bresnahan putting on the gear. Note the primitive shin guards.*

● *New York Giants manager John McGraw (center) and two of the great pitchers that Bresnahan handled, Christy Mathewson (left) and "Iron Man" Joe McGinnity.*

with several others including manager John McGraw, he made a midseason leap back to the National League, joining the New York Giants. (It wasn't until 1903 that the rival leagues came to agreement and stopped pirating each other's players.)

John McGraw began his long reign as Giants manager in 1902 and for the first few years played Bresnahan in the outfield, a position that was compatible with Roger's running speed and strong arm. In 1903, Roger had his best year ever, batting .350. In 1905, he began catching and quickly became a favorite of Giant ace Christy Mathewson, who said that his new batterymate was "as brainy as he is tough." The

Giants won the pennant that year and Bresnahan played in his only World Series, batting .313 as the Giants won in five games. This was the famous "all-shutout" Series, when every game ended in a blanking. Bresnahan called the shots as Mathewson fired three shutouts and Joe McGinnity one for the winners.

After just a few years behind the plate, Bresnahan had established himself as the best in the game. One contemporary writer, in the flourishes of the day, had this to say about the Giants star:

> Watch him while he is catching. Watch him throw to bases. Absolute, unerring decision is his. Never a moment of hesitation, a second of doubt. He

● *A rare action photo from baseball's early days. That's Bresnahan behind the plate and Honus Wagner at bat.*

heaves that ball to second or to third or to first as the lightning chance may demand, with a sort of cold, infallible ferocity. And he possesses that alacrity of taking a chance, that audacity which differentiates soldiers of genius from the prudent plodder who, maneuvering beautifully, loses battles with skill and grace.

It was in 1907 that Bresnahan made the contribution for which the catching fraternity has been ever grateful. Incredible as it seems today, catchers in those years worked under the bat with no more protective gear than a primitive mask and chest protector. Bresnahan got the idea for shin guards from watching a game of cricket, in which the bowlers wore protection on their shins. Thus inspired, and tired of living all summer with aching shinbones, Roger decided that a baseball player could be as smart as a cricketeer.

"I didn't invent anything," Roger said in a 1926 interview. "I simply got a pair of shin guards, such as cricket players wore, and I strapped them outside my stockings. I was sick and tired of wild pitches, foul balls, thrown bats, and flying spikes bruising and cutting my legs."

At first the innovation was greeted with derision—Bresnahan endured taunts and catcalls of "sissy"—but other catchers soon saw the wisdom of wearing this extra protection, and within a few years shin guards became a standard feature of every catcher's protective equipment.

Bresnahan spent his off-seasons in his native Toledo, where he worked as a private detective. He took great pride in his sleuthing abilities (no player of his, he claimed when he later managed, could ever get away with breaking curfew). This pride was slightly dampened, however, when he returned to his hotel in New York one evening

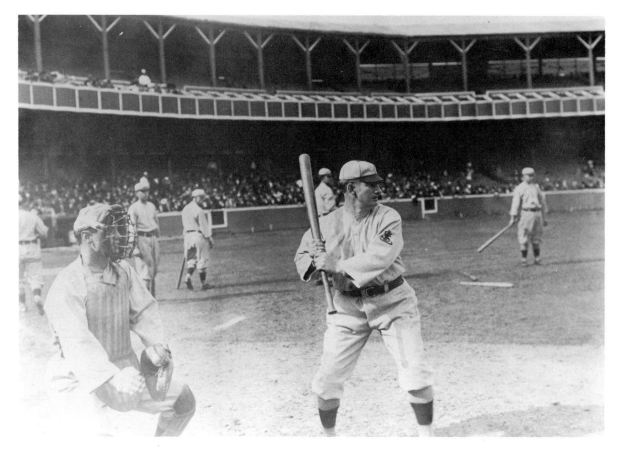

● *Bresnahan with the Cardinals in 1910. It was not unusual for batters to choke-up on the bat so severely in the dead-ball era.*

and discovered that some light-fingered Louie in the jostling crowds had picked his pockets clean.

After the 1908 season, the St. Louis Cardinals told McGraw they wanted his star catcher as player-manager. Knowing of Roger's desire to manage and not wanting to stand in the way of opportunity, McGraw swung a deal that sent Bresnahan to St. Louis (McGraw was able to be so accommodating because he had the estimable Chief Meyers ready to replace Bresnahan).

Bresnahan managed the Cardinals to four second-division finishes from 1909–1912 and then talked himself out of the job, literally. After

the 1912 season he was summoned to the home of the club owner for a conference on how to improve the team. The owner was Mrs. Helene Robison Britton, who had inherited the franchise from her father and was the first female club owner in baseball history. She was a tough-minded woman, an outspoken advocate of women's rights; she also took a lively interest in her club. When she voiced some criticisms of the team and outlined her suggestions for improving things, Bresnahan began simmering. He soon boiled over. What, he asked in indelicate language, did a woman know about baseball, and where did she come off telling Roger Bresnahan

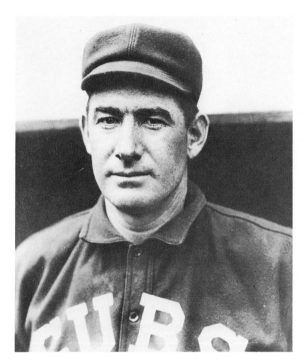

● *Bresnahan with the Cubs in 1915, his last year in the majors.*

about the game? It was impolite to use such language and display such an attitude to a woman, and when the woman was also the one who signed the checks, inadvisable.

Despite being in the middle of a $10,000 per year contract (generous for the time), Bresnahan found himself canned by the incensed Mrs. Britton.

After some squabbling over his contract, Roger was sold to the Cubs, for whom he played for several years and managed in 1915, his last year as an active player in the big leagues. Bresnahan then bought his hometown club, the Toledo Mud Hens of the American Association and managed it until 1923, when he disposed of his interests. (During his ownership, the local writers couldn't resist calling the team "The Bresna Hens.")

Bresnahan later returned to the majors as a coach for McGraw from 1925 through 1928 and then for the Detroit Tigers in the early 1930s, after which time he left baseball.

Bresnahan died on December 4, 1944, two months before his election to the Hall of Fame.

Johnny Kling.

JOHNNY KLING

For those who watched the games and kept the scorebooks for the first quarter of the twentieth century, there were over that considerable box of time but two catchers in the National League: Roger Bresnahan and Johnny Kling. But since the heyday of Kling ran roughly from 1902 through 1908 there are no longer reliable eyewitnesses to tell us whether Johnny's glittering reputation as a catcher was entirely justified. And so we must take that reputation on faith and be believers in the echoes of unheard cheers.

Kling caught for the Chicago Cub teams that won pennants in 1906, 1907, 1908, and 1910, with the 1906 club setting an all-time record with 116 wins. These were the teams of Joe Tinker, Johnny Evers, and Frank Chance, baseball's most famous double play makers (thanks in large part to a dubious piece of poetry by New York newspaperman Franklin P. Adams that made them sound like a brick wall around the infield). But these were also the teams of pitchers Mordecai (Three Finger) Brown, Jack Pfiester, Ed Reulbach, and Orval Overall, a staff that regularly posted stunningly low earned-run averages, low even for that dead-ball era when the bunt and the stolen base were key offensive weapons.

"They are all very good pitchers," John McGraw said of the Cub mound corps, "but the man who makes them go is Kling."

Brown, ace of the Chicago staff and for years the one pitcher in the league who was a match for New York's Christy Mathewson, was lavish in praise of his batterymate, lauding Johnny's brains, arm, and ruggedness (Kling, like his contemporaries, played much of his career before Bresnahan's introduction of shin guards).

"I'm not ashamed to admit," Brown once said, "that I was just a so-so pitcher before I teamed up with Kling. A pitcher can always tell you how good a catcher is, and take my word: Johnny Kling was the best."

Kling stood up at 5'9½" and weighed around 160 pounds, not very imposing by current standards but average for his time. He was born in Kansas City, Missouri, on February 25, 1875, son of a German-born baker. Cut from old-world cloth, Kling's father thought baseball was a waste of time and forbade young Johnny from

● *The famous infield that made baseball history in turn-of-the-century Chicago. (Left to right), third baseman Harry Steinfeldt, shortstop Joe Tinker, second baseman Johnny Evers, first baseman (and manager) Frank Chance.*

playing. Talent, however, will always create its own tides and find its own outlets, and so under the name of "Kline" the boy began playing semi-pro ball around Kansas City. When Kling senior found out about it and found out, too, that young Johnny was being paid five dollars a game, the old man relented.

Kling's bullet-throwing arm and defensive skills soon got him into pro ball with the Emporia, Kansas, club. He later played for Rockford, Illinois, Houston, and then St. Joseph in the Western Association, from whom he was purchased by the Cubs at the end of the 1900 season.

Kling's main rival for the Chicago catching job was young Frank Chance, but by 1902 the job belonged to Johnny, and Chance was put on first base, the foundation blocks for what was to become the most dominant team in the league.

In those years, with men on first and third, the steal of second was almost automatic, as few catchers were willing to run the risk of throwing through, lest the man on third come home. With

● *The great Three Finger Brown, who said, "I'm not ashamed to admit that I was just a so-so pitcher before I teamed up with Kling."*

his powerful arm, however, Kling began challenging the man going to second.

"His throws were sharp and on the money," second baseman Evers recalled. "The pegs were so fast that we were not only able to stop all but the fastest runners, but the men on third soon realized they didn't have time to make it home."

"Tinker, Evers, and Chance were great in the infield," Mordecai Brown said, "but Kling deserved plenty of credit too. He kept those baserunners nailed to the spot." And those "nailed" baserunners helped the Cub staff to its record-breaking earned-run averages: 2.04 in 1905, 1.76 in 1906, 1.73 in 1907, each a league low.

Johnny doubled his value with some solid hitting, with averages of .312, .284, and .276 in the pennant years of 1906 to 1908, outhitting Bresnahan, his only rival for catching supremacy during those years.

One of Johnny's brothers ran a poolroom in Kansas City and the ace catcher spent much of his off-season time there polishing another of his skills. In the winter of 1908, Kling proved good enough to win the pocket billiard championship of the world (tacking it onto the championship the Cubs had won in the recent World Series). When his pool table victory coincided with a salary squabble with Cubs owner Charles Murphy, Johnny decided to retire from baseball and concentrate on bumping balls around a billiard table.

So Kling sat out the 1909 season, defending his green cloth table title. In his absence the Cubs failed to win the pennant after three straight triumphs. Murphy was so incensed by what he termed Kling's "betrayal" that he denounced his catcher and fined him $700, to be paid if and when Johnny returned.

Kling thumbed his nose at Murphy and the fine, but when he lost his pocket billiard title in 1909, Johnny returned to the Cubs. The implacable Murphy refused to rescind the fine and so it cost Kling $700 to return to baseball.

With their great catcher on the job once more, the Cubs won the pennant in 1910, making it four in a row for Kling (omitting the season he had missed). But pennant or no pennant, Murphy remained unforgiving about Johnny's one-year defection and early in the 1911 season traded his now thirty-six-year-old catcher to the Boston Braves.

Kling managed the Braves in 1912 (finishing last), catching half the games and batting .317, his career high. He wrapped up his thirteen-year big league career with Cincinnati the following season.

Returning to Kansas City, Johnny operated several pool halls and later ran the Kansas City team in the American Association, selling out his interests to the New York Yankees in 1937.

Always as clever with a buck as he was with a pitched ball, Kling was reportedly a millionaire when he died in the city he had always called home, on January 31, 1947.

How good was Johnny Kling? Just how snappy were those throws that sizzled across the old ball fields of long ago? If we take on faith the consensus of opinion of bygone witnesses, then it becomes as close to fact as can be that the wiry little man from Kansas City who "nailed" baserunners with stunning effect and brainstormed a gifted pitching staff into the record books was indeed one of the best.

● *Kling with Boston in 1912.*

Ray Schalk: "crisp and businesslike, on the field and off."

RAY SCHALK

I t is true, in the main, when people say that if you associate with bad company you run the risk of having your good name besmirched. This good old shank of wisdom, however, did not hold true for Ray Schalk, who (through no choosing of his own) associated with a band of gifted rogues, and when he emerged from the experience untainted, it made him look even more virtuous than he already was.

Schalk happened to be the catcher on the 1919 Chicago White Sox, a team that was as crooked as it was talented, which was plenty in both columns. When it came to arranging the infamous fix of the World Series, the various gamblers and White Sox players who were involved knew better than to ask Schalk to participate in the swindle.

"You looked at him," one Chicago writer said, "and you saw a man who bristled with integrity. He was crisp and businesslike, on the field and off. I think that's how he got that nickname." The nickname was "Cracker."

Ray (Cracker) Schalk was born in the farmland community of Harvel, Illinois, population 500, on August 12, 1892. Sixty-three years later, his name became prominent in another small

American town, Cooperstown, New York. Only three twentieth century catchers had made the Hall of Fame ahead of him: Roger Bresnahan (1945), Mickey Cochrane (1947), and Bill Dickey (1954). Schalk was inducted the same year as Gabby Hartnett.

It was more than integrity that enabled Schalk to attain the pinnacle of his profession. Until the emergence of Cochrane and Dickey in the late 1920s, Schalk was considered the top catcher in American League history, a span of nearly three decades. Contemporaries like Wally Schang and Steve O'Neill might outhit Schalk by as much as 40 or 50 points in a season, but this was more than offset, in general opinion, by what Schalk did behind the plate.

"If you went to the plate and tried to guess with him," said longtime White Sox pitcher Red Faber, "you were out of luck. Ray had a pattern of calling for pitches unlike any other catcher's. When it came to running a ball game, there was nobody like him."

● *Right-hander Red Faber, who won 254 games for the White Sox, said of Schalk, "When it came to running a ball game, there was nobody like him."*

Schalk won his acclaim despite unprepossessing size (around 5'7" and 155 pounds) and modest lifetime average (.253). His personal high was .282 and altogether he popped just twelve home runs in a career that ran from 1912 to 1929, with his truly active days ending in 1926.

By 1916 Schalk was already recognized as the league's best catcher. The White Sox at this time were putting together the team that would win pennants in 1917 and 1919 and that by all accounts would have won a few more if not for the nefarious business of the 1919 World Series,

which resulted in eight of their players, including the great Shoeless Joe Jackson, being booted out of organized ball.

After describing the superb attributes of Jackson, second baseman Eddie Collins (not involved in the scandal), and the rest of the burgeoning White Sox club, one writer said, "But the one element of strength which knits together all the rest is undoubtedly the keen brain, breadth of judgment, and strength of throwing arm of Ray Schalk, the greatest catcher in the American League."

The little man also possessed another invaluable asset for a catcher: durability; he caught over one hundred games for eleven consecutive seasons and twelve overall, a league record Dickey broke by one. Schalk set and still holds major league records for most years leading in putouts (nine), most years leading in fielding (eight), and the American League record for lifetime assists (1,810).

Ray's original ambition in life was to become a printer, and when still a teenager he went to Brooklyn to study the operation of the linotype machine; but when he had completed his course and returned home he found his opportunities limited. What the printing profession lost, baseball gained. Always a catcher, he began putting his talents to work on the semipro diamonds of Illinois, earning two bucks a game. Soon he was behind the plate for Taylorville, an entry in the Illinois-Missouri League. Progress was swift; in the middle of his first season, 1911, the Milwaukee club (then in the American Association) bought him, and by the end of the 1912 season he was with Chicago.

Schalk made an immediate impression on his new teammates, one of whom recalled the twenty-year-old rookie's first game, catching the veteran spitballer Ed Walsh (the spitball was still a legal pitch then).

"Walsh was pitching at the time with all his old speed and strength," the teammate said. "The spitball is notoriously hard to catch, and Schalk being new to the game had difficulty in getting Walsh to read his signals. Finally he said to Walsh, 'Never mind any more signals, just cut

● " . . . the greatest catcher in the American League."

● Ed Walsh.

loose with whatever you want and I will hold you,' and he did. That was some stunt for any catcher, let alone a youngster just breaking into the league.''

Ted Lyons, who joined the White Sox in 1923 and pitched until 1946, remembered the first words of advice he received when reaching the big leagues straight off the campus of Baylor University.

They told me to listen to Ray Schalk. Well, I was a smart college kid with a good fastball, and I said, "Why?" Because, they told me, if anybody could make a big league pitcher out of me, it was Ray Schalk. And you know, they were right. He'd come out to the mound during the game and tell me what to throw and where. I would ask him why. "Because I know what the batter is thinking," he'd say. I'd laugh and say, "All right, Ray." I never asked him how he knew, but I guess he did, because he was right far more times than he was wrong. In all my years in baseball I never saw a smarter or more competent catcher.

With Schalk taking charge of the pitching staff, the White Sox won the pennant in 1917 and beat the Giants in the World Series, impressing Giants manager John McGraw. "It's that little man behind the plate," McGraw said after the Series, "that's where they get it all from. I don't care how good a team is, they can't win without brain power, and Schalk generates most of it for them."

Again in 1919, it was Schalk's masterful handling of a talented staff that led the Sox to the World Series, but this time it was a painful experience for him, for he could see that ace pitchers Eddie Cicotte and Lefty Williams were not trying to win; they would not throw the pitches he called for. Schalk railed at them, but there was little he could do.

The White Sox were on their way to another flag in 1920 when the scandal broke in the season's final weeks, leading to the suspension of most of the team's stars.

His teammates' treachery left Schalk heartbroken and he seldom spoke of the 1919 club.

"A lot of things bothered him about that mess," Lyons said. "The betrayal, of course, hurt the most. And the harm it did to baseball. And the money it cost him, because by all accounts that team was going to be in the World Series a few more times."

In 1920, Schalk set a record by becoming the first catcher to catch over 150 games in a season (151), and through the 1920s he continued to set endurance records.

"I'll tell you what made him so tough," the White Sox trainer of the day said.

It was desire. Remember, most catchers were built like ice-wagons; Ray looked like a frail little guy. One afternoon a red hot foul tip struck him on the collarbone. It not only knocked him down, it knocked him out. We had to work over him for some time, resorting to artificial respiration and the use of oxygen. As soon as he got his breath and collected his senses, he immediately wanted to get behind the plate. Later, after the game, I laughed and said to him, "Ray, just what does it need to knock you out of a game?" He gave me a stern look and said, "They haven't found it yet."

After the scandal broke them apart, the White Sox became a sluggish second-division club for the rest of Schalk's career, removing the brilliant little catcher from the limelight. Schalk managed the club in 1927 and half of 1928, with little success. He wrapped up his active career with the Giants in 1929, getting into just five games.

Schalk died in Chicago, on May 19, 1970, with the satisfaction of Hall of Fame recognition, but also with the gnawing resentment of having had his career mugged at its very height by his maneuvering teammates, the notorious "Eight Men Out."

● *White Sox manager Ray Schalk in 1927.*

Gabby Hartnett in 1923.

GABBY HARTNETT

Paul Richards had been on the big league scene for more than half a century, as player, manager, and front office executive, building a reputation as a shrewd, objective observer of talent, one whose opinions were generally deferred to, particularly when it came to catchers, the position he himself had played. Once, when asked his assessment of the catchers he had seen, he included the following:

"The best throwing arm I ever saw on a catcher probably belonged to Gabby Hartnett. And he was accurate. He was just a great throwing catcher. Better than Johnny Bench? Yes. The fans used to come out early to watch infield practice just to watch Hartnett throw the ball around. That's quite a tribute to a fellow's throwing arm, wouldn't you say?"

The tribute may be expanded: Until the arrival of Johnny Bench, Hartnett was incontestably the greatest catcher in National League history. Along with that theatrical throwing arm, Gabby had top-shelf defensive abilities (he led league catchers in fielding six times), and a solid bat (.297 lifetime average).

He was born Charles Leo Hartnett, on December 20, 1900, in Woonsocket, Rhode Island, and was raised in Millville, Massachusetts, just outside of Boston. He was one of fourteen children of a streetcar conductor who had also been a good semipro ballplayer and who encouraged his talented son to play baseball. "I was lucky," Hartnett said in later years. "I had good instruction from day one."

His teammates called him Leo, but to the press and baseball public at large Hartnett was "Gabby," the nickname handed to him by a Chicago sportswriter.

"He called me that," Hartnett said, "because we sat together on the train going to my first spring training and I never said a word. You see, I was taking my mother's advice; she had told me to keep my mouth shut until I saw what was going on. It was good advice, too."

Once he felt comfortable in the big leagues, however, Hartnett became a veritable chatterbox, with a winning

● *"Until the arrival of Johnny Bench, Hartnett was incontestably the greatest catcher in National League history."*

personality and a politician's broad, disarming smile.

Along with that convincing throwing arm and the all-around talent that got him into the Hall of Fame in 1955, along with his natural charm and rascal's grin, Gabby also logged a singular achievement at Wrigley Field one darkening late September afternoon in 1938 when he struck the most resounding home run in Chicago Cubs history and one of the most memorable ever in all of baseball. It was the kind of home run that assures a man a niche on the wall of legend, the

kind of home run for which destiny sets the table and waits for someone to make a feast of it. Hartnett's storybook home run came in a double twilight—both an afternoon and a career were enwreathed in shadows.

Hartnett's career began professionally in 1921, when he joined the Worcester, Massachusetts, club in the Eastern League. The young man batted .264 and was so impressive behind the plate the Chicago Cubs snapped up his contract for all of $2,500 and covered his erect 6'11" frame with the big league uniform he was to wear for the next 19 years.

Hartnett made his big league debut with the Cubs in 1922, catching no one less than Grover Cleveland Alexander, a man whose impeccable mound artistry was by then legendary. Alex was impressed, describing the rookie as "a smart kid" who had "a very good arm." (That arm again; one begins to think it came from an ordnance factory.) As far as Hartnett was concerned, he never again saw pitching as inspiring as Alexander's. "Alex was the greatest I ever caught throwing at three different speeds," he said. "He was the greatest I ever caught, period."

The Cubs already had one of the league's top catchers in Bob O'Farrell, and now they suddenly realized they had a youngster who was going to be even better. Early in the 1925 season, O'Farrell was traded to the Cardinals and Hartnett took over the regular spot, soon becoming the league's top catcher as well as one of its most colorful personalities.

"He was 'Gabby' all right," said Joe McCarthy, who managed the Cubs from 1926 through 1930 (and who felt Hartnett was superior to Mickey Cochrane and Bill Dickey as an all-around catcher). "It wasn't that he talked so much, though he did chatter a lot, but because he was always yelling at his infielders and pitcher during the game. That was his way of hustling while sitting still. Sometimes, if he felt the pitcher wasn't bearing down enough, he'd fire the ball back to the mound like a rifle shot. That caught the fellow's attention, believe me."

● *Grover Cleveland Alexander.*

● *Hartnett in the mid-1930s.*

Hartnett's darkest time as a player came in 1929, when that famous arm suddenly went dead. The injury held him to just twenty-five games, most of them as a pinch-hitter. (In spite of losing their star catcher, a hard-hitting Cubs team won the pennant anyway.)

In 1930, Gabby's arm restored itself to its old strength and he turned in a powerhouse season, batting .339 and achieving personal highs with thirty-seven home runs and 122 runs batted in, setting power-hitting records for catchers that stood for many years.

With Hartnett behind the plate, the Cubs were one of the National League's muscle teams of the 1930s, winning pennants in 1932, 1935, and 1938. In 1935 he sparked the team to the pennant with a .344 batting average and was voted the league's Most Valuable Player. Two years later, at the age of thirty-seven, he reached a career high with a .354 batting average (the only National League catcher ever to bat higher was the Giant's Chief Meyers with .358 in 1912). His career already rich in honors and awards,

Gabby's most stellar moment was still to come, in 1938, his seventeenth year in the major leagues.

On July 20, 1938, Hartnett was suddenly elevated to the Cubs managerial job, replacing Charlie Grimm. The team was in third place when Gabby took over, with a clear shot at the pennant, a pennant that the new skipper would take a personal and dramatic hand in winning.

As the 1938 season ran to its final games, the Cubs were dueling the Pittsburgh Pirates for first place. On September 17, the Cubs were three and a half games behind, creating such confidence in Pittsburgh that the Pirate management began enlarging their press box and turning out souvenir pins for the anticipated World Series (those pins have long since been choice items on the collector's market).

On September 27, the Pirate lead was one and a half games with Pittsburgh invading Wrigley Field for a three-game shootout. The Cubs won the opener behind the gutty pitching of sore-armed Dizzy Dean, trimming the Pirate margin to the thinnest of slices, a half game. The following day Gabby Hartnett shot a home run that only Hollywood could have blushed and conjured.

Going into the bottom of the ninth inning, the score was tied, 5–5, darkness was settling quickly over Wrigley Field (without lights in those days), and a doubleheader seemed likely for the next day (the umpires had already indicated this would be the last inning), a prospect that disheartened Hartnett, whose pitching staff had been worked overtime coming down the stretch.

On the mound for Pittsburgh was their ace reliever, right-hander Mace Brown, who was about to become the unwilling accomplice to a loud moment of baseball history.

Brown retired the first two Chicago batters, then faced Hartnett (a man described by McCarthy as the best clutch hitter he had ever seen).

Gabby swung at Brown's first delivery and missed. The next one he ticked foul. The game was now just one strike off from being filed away as a tie. Brown's next pitch was intended to break low and away, the pitcher said, but the curveball swooped right across the plate and Hartnett swung where he believed it was, because, he said later, "It was so dark I could hardly follow the damn thing."

But the moment he made contact, Gabby knew. "I got the kind of feeling you get when the blood rushes to your head and you get dizzy," he said. "I knew it was gone." Gabby knew it before anyone else did (although Brown later said that the sound of the bat hitting the ball "made me immediately sick") because in the diminished visibility it was difficult to follow the flight of the ball.

The ball carried through the graying air on a high, ringing line and dropped into the left-field seats to become one of baseball's magical home runs, one of those historical moments that never needs resurrection because it never truly perishes. It became, in baseball lore, "the homer in the gloamin'."

When they realized what had happened, over 34,000 Wrigley Field partisans began whooping and hollering, and by the time Gabby reached second base they were spilling out onto the field, forcing the hero to battle his way around the bases and follow a flying wedge of teammates to home plate.

The stunning victory put the Cubs on top by a half game, and the following day they trampled a demoralized Pirate team by a 10–1 score and went on to take the pennant.

After this high-water mark, which came so late in his career, Gabby's descent was fairly quick. On November 13, 1940, the catcher-manager was released by the Cubs, closing out his nineteen-year career in Chicago. Signing on as a player-coach with the New York Giants, the forty-year-old Hartnett played one year, got into

● *Pittsburgh's Mace Brown, who threw the famous home run ball.*

● *Hartnett with the New York Giants in 1941, his final big league season.*

sixty-four games, batted an even .300, hit the last of his 236 home runs, and left as the all-time record-holder for games caught, 1,790.

Gabby later managed in the minor leagues for several years, then left baseball in 1946 and operated a bowling alley in suburban Chicago. He had a last, brief job in a baseball uniform as a coach with the Kansas City Athletics in 1965.

Hartnett's cycle through the years was perfectly rounded—born on December 20, 1900, he died on December 20, 1972.

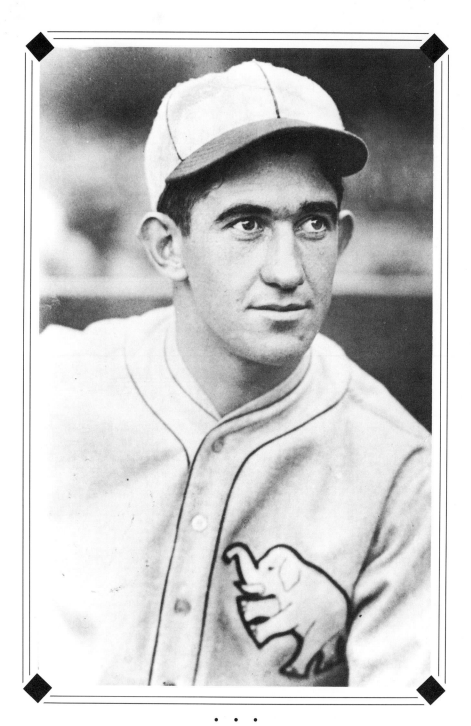

Mickey Cochrane, perennial candidate for baseball's
all-time catcher.

MICKEY COCHRANE

Traditionally, the careers of superstars come to a close with endings mellow and poignant, with wistful memories of the old strength and speed that once were. Sometimes the retiring giant makes his last trip around the schedule almost ceremonial, the occasions awash with sentiment. But Mickey Cochrane had none of that. The end of his career came with the shocking suddenness of a shootout at high noon.

It was the afternoon of May 25, 1937, a day alive with warm spring sunshine, a good day for a ball game. The Detroit Tigers, led by their catcher-manager Mickey Cochrane, were playing the Yankees in New York's famous stadium in the Bronx. The afternoon's warmth induced the shedding of jackets, creating in the center field bleachers a vexing background of white shirts. For the batters, the day's work became difficult and hazardous; picking up the pitch was like trying to spot an aspirin tablet on a white bedsheet. And on this particular day, the tablet was moving very fast.

The hard-throwing Irving (Bump) Hadley was on the mound for the Yankees, Cochrane was at the plate. With a man on first, Hadley was working from a set position. Charlie Gehringer, the on-deck hitter, was just a few feet away.

"It was a high inside pitch," Gehringer said. "Mickey never saw it. He didn't even flinch. The ball hit him in the head so hard it bounced straight back to Hadley. Cochrane went down like he'd been hit with an axe." (Cochrane later said he had lost track of the ball in the white-shirted background the moment it left Hadley's hand.)

His skull fractured in three places, Cochrane drifted in and out of consciousness for ten days.

"That blow," one of Cochrane's doctors said, "might well have killed a lesser man."

Well, they had been saying for years how tough Mickey Cochrane was, behind the plate, with his fists, in his all-around relentless style of play. "Tough?" teammate Doc Cramer said of Mickey. "Like a piece of flint. Usually, when a baserunner is barreling into the plate you feel sorry for the catcher. But with Mickey, you felt sorry for the runner. He was about to hit a brick wall. Because Mickey believed

● *When they said "play ball," he stopped smiling.*

home plate belonged to him, you see. You had to take it away from him."

Tough, aggressive, determined: the words resonate through the Mickey Cochrane story, from the very beginning, which was on April 3, 1903, in Bridgewater, Massachusetts, a town some fifty miles south of Boston.

"By the time he was ten years old," a childhood friend remembered, "you were taking notice of him. It seemed he was always marching off to the baseball field, a bat over his shoulder with a glove hanging from it. He was big for his age and broad-shouldered, with a shock of unruly black hair and a very determined look in his eyes."

What was this tough little mug thinking about at age ten? A baseball career, of course; but even more. "A lot of kids want to be big-league *players*," he told sportswriter Frank Graham in 1955, "but I don't know of another who looked beyond that to a *manager's* job. How did I happen to think of it? Who knows? What makes kids think of things? Maybe I just had to be the boss."

Translate "boss" into leadership and you had the quintessential Mickey Cochrane. He had the flair, the guts, and the ability, and of course the desire. He was an athletic legend at Boston University in the early 1920s, the greatest athlete in the university's history, so the old timers claimed. He starred on the ball field, the gridiron, the basketball court, the cinder track, and in the ring, where he boxed at 160 pounds and could deflate you with either hand.

Cochrane entered professional baseball in 1923, with the Dover, Delaware, club of the Eastern Shore League. In sixty-five games he batted .322 while impressing everyone with his blazing style of play. In those years most minor league clubs were independently owned (sustaining themselves by developing good young players and selling them to the majors or higher minors), and after the season Dover sold its young catcher to Portland of the Pacific Coast League. The Coast League being the fastest of the minors, this was a sizeable jump, but Cochrane achieved it with room to spare, batting .333 for Portland in 1924.

Tales of Mickey's incandescent abilities reached the attentive ears of Connie Mack, skipper and part owner of the Philadelphia Athletics. Mack was diligently rebuilding a once-championship club that had finished last from 1915 through 1921 and which in 1924 had raised itself to the more respectable precincts of fifth place. Connie had just added to his employment rolls youngsters named Jimmie Foxx, Lefty Grove, and Al Simmons, and now for $50,000—heavy bucks for a minor leaguer back then—he enrolled Cochrane.

"He was worth it," said Connie years later. "In fact, he was worth ten times that much. More than any other player, he was responsible for the pennants we won in 1929, 1930, and 1931."

A weakness on pop fouls kept the new man on the bench on opening day in 1925, Mack going with his smooth veteran Cy Perkins.

"But only until the eighth inning," Perkins recalled.

● *Connie Mack (center) has his arms around the greatest battery in baseball history, Cochrane (left) and Lefty Grove.*

"We were down a few runs, had a couple of men on and Mr. Mack sent the kid up to hit for me. Mickey lined a double into right-center and I knew I'd lost my job. It wasn't just that he got the hit, it was the way he tore around first and roared into second. The dirt was flying around him. It was like letting a lion out of the cage. But I didn't mind. When somebody as good as Mickey Cochrane comes along, you just sit back and enjoy the privilege of watching him.

Athletics third baseman Jimmy Dykes remembered when Cochrane broke the seal.

"I thought we had a rookie there," Dykes said with a laugh. "You know, rookies are supposed to keep their mouths shut and learn. But this kid took right over. He was a ball of fire from the get-go. If he didn't think a pitcher was bearing down hard enough, he'd go out there and tell him so. Even Grove."

Even Grove. Robert Moses (Lefty) Grove, the greatest left-handed pitcher then in captivity, and perhaps the greatest ever. The tempestuous, cantankerous Grove fired creation's most searing fastball, and the only thing hotter was Lefty's temper, his will to win (described by one witness as "terrifying"). Although the great Grove seldom needed any prodding from anyone, when he did, Cochrane was not shy about giving it.

> Cochrane once said in an interview, a catcher's best work appears not so much in what he does, as in what never happens. That sounds a little involved and not too sensible. But it's the truth. Here's an illustration. A pitcher may be on the ragged edge, just ready to blow up. A good catcher knows it. He knows how to handle that pitcher, how to steady him, how to help him over a tight spot. The pitcher doesn't blow up. He settles down and pitches a beautiful ball game. Does anyone remember that point back there in the early innings, it may be, when he was so near the showers that he could almost feel them spatter on him? No, that's all forgotten. Perhaps not one spectator in ten even realized it at that time. It was one of those things that might have happened, but didn't.

His teammates were quick to accept Mickey's zealous leadership, and the fact that the rookie catcher batted .331 in his first season no doubt helped firm up that acceptance.

When comparing Cochrane and his contemporary, the Yankees' Bill Dickey—for decades it was one of baseball's favorite parlor games—the pro-Cochrane faction was always quick to point out, with no argument, Mickey's superior running speed. The former track star and halfback from Boston U. could fly around the bases like few catchers ever could, and on occasion Mack even used him in the lead-off spot.

By 1929, the Philadelphia Athletics were ready to replace Babe Ruth's Yankees as the American League's dominant team. It was truly a clash of titans—if the 1927 Yankees were not baseball's premier all-time team, then the 1929 to 1931 A's, in the opinion of many, were.

In the pennant years Cochrane batted .331, .357, and .349. With Grove pitching to records of 28–5 and 31–4 in 1930 and 1931, the two men formed what is beyond question the greatest battery in baseball history. (Fittingly, Gordon Stanley Cochrane and Robert Moses Grove entered the Hall of Fame as a single entry in 1947.)

The 1929 World Series between the Athletics and Chicago Cubs was a contest between a couple of hard-boiled teams. The A's were better and proved it, winning in five games. But the Cubs were their equals in loud and profane bench-jockeying. The exchanges became so sulphurous, with the decibel count reaching into the stands, that Commissioner Landis felt it necessary to intervene. He summoned the opposing managers, Mack and Chicago's Joe McCarthy, and ordered them to have the language laundered and the volume turned down. The skippers passed the word along.

When the next game began, Cochrane headed out to his place behind the plate, paused, looked into the Cub dugout and yelled, "Come on out, boys. Put on your bib and tucker. We're serving tea and cookies today." After the A's had won the Series, Landis went to their clubhouse to offer congratulations. When he got to Cochrane, the fearsome Landis put on a mock scowl and said, "Tea and cookies, eh?" The abashed Cochrane smiled and shrugged. "You heard me, huh?" he said. "For Christ's sake," Landis laughed, "you said it loud enough."

The A's won the Series again in 1930, but in 1931 they, and Cochrane in particular, ran up against a Cardinal rookie named Pepper Martin. It was Pepper's Series; he batted .500 and ran wild, stealing five bases. Martin's performance left Cochrane seething, since most fans blame a stolen base on the catcher. Baseball people knew better.

● *Cochrane (right) greeting St. Louis Cardinal catcher Gus Mancuso during the 1931 World Series.*

● *The Tiger skipper in 1934.*

"Blaming Cochrane was pure nonsense," said Cardinal pitcher Bill Hallahan, who had witnessed Pepper's depradations. "Pepper was stealing on the pitchers—most bases are stolen on the pitcher. You give a catcher like Cochrane a chance to throw you out and he's going to do it." Nevertheless, Mickey became the "goat" of the Athletics' seven-game loss in the 1931 World Series.

After 1931, Mack, who had sustained heavy losses in the stock market crash and was now seeing his club's attendance falling off sharply, began selling off his high-salaried stars. In December 1933, Cochrane was sold to the Detroit Tigers for $100,000.

Appointed manager of the Tigers, Cochrane quickly galvanized a strong club and breathed into it the fire needed to win. The Tigers had some sterling talent that included second baseman Charlie Gehringer, first baseman Hank Greenberg, outfielder Goose Goslin, and pitchers Schoolboy Rowe and Tommy Bridges.

According to Greenberg, "Cochrane was the spark that ignited us. He was an inspirational leader. . . . There was an intangible something about him, a winning spirit, that was really infectious."

The infection took hold and became teamwide. Cochrane brought home pennant winners in his first two years with Detroit, 1934 and 1935, the club's first champions since 1909, giving Mickey the personal distinction of playing on five pennant winners in seven years.

● Pepper Martin, who bedeviled Cochrane in the 1931 World Series, is doing it again during the 1934 Series. Here's Pepper belly-whopping home in the sixth inning of Game 1, while Cochrane awaits the throw that never came. The umpire is Brick Owens.

● Former Detroit star Ty Cobb (center) saying hello to Cochrane (left) and Charlie Gehringer.

● *Cochrane being carried off the field after the Hadley beaning at Yankee Stadium on May 25, 1937.*

The Tigers came up short in the 1934 Series, losing in seven to Dizzy Dean and the Cardinal "Gashouse Gang," but a year later it was different. In 1935, Cochrane led the Detroit charge over the Cubs and brought the franchise its first world championship.

At that point, the world seemed bright and petal-strewn for Cochrane. He was thirty-two years old, manager of the world champions, hailed by many as the greatest of all catchers. A man to be admired and envied. But it evidently was all too sweet for some palate somewhere, for soon thunderclouds clashed over his head and the world of Mickey Cochrane spun into gloom.

In 1936, the intense Cochrane suffered a nervous breakdown during the season and played in just forty-four games. Fully recovered, he was back in 1937, but twenty-seven games into the season Bump Hadley's fastball came flashing out of the white shirts of Yankee Stadium and Cochrane's playing days were over. (Typically, Mickey wanted to return to action after recovering from the beaning, but Detroit management, fearing that another such blow could be fatal, forbade it.)

Strictly a bench manager now, Cochrane was unhappy. With this forced inactivity came a banking of the famous Cochrane fires.

"He wasn't happy being just a manager," Gehringer said. "You could see it. He was still young enough to be playing and all of that nervous energy had nowhere to go. It ate him up."

In August 1938 the Tigers fired Cochrane.

The great catcher's most fulfilling post-career years came during the war. Commissioned a lieutenant-commander, he was assigned to the Great Lakes Naval Training Station as athletic director, his duties including coaching a very talented team of former major leaguers.

Cochrane died on June 28, 1962, at Lake Forest, Illinois. He was fifty-nine years old.

Mickey Cochrane had been blessed with many gifts; his hitting, running, and throwing were the visible ones; he also possessed those priceless intangibles—his invincible spirit and determination and will to win. The fire that burned within Mickey Cochrane was a remarkably bright one, with a glow that reached far and warmed many an imagination. We know that it reached as far as the tiny Oklahoma mining town of Spavinaw, for when his first son was born on October 20, 1931, lead and zinc miner Mutt Mantle named the boy Mickey, after his favorite player.

● *Bump Hadley.*

Bill Dickey in 1929, his first full year as a Yankee.

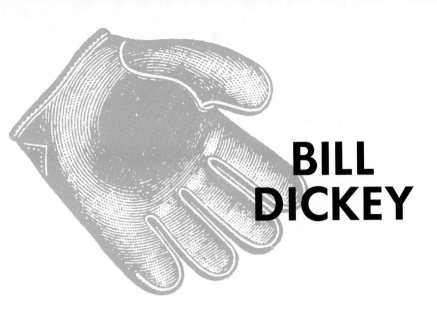

BILL DICKEY

Fate, destiny, chance—the mighty engines of determination do not involve themselves only with the fortunes of nations and empires. Take, for instance, the tire on Blake Harper's automobile. Who was Blake Harper? Well, he was, in 1925, the president of the Fort Smith, Arkansas, club of the Southern Association. One day that summer, at the behest of St. Louis Cardinals general manager Branch Rickey, he was driving to Hot Springs to sign a good-looking young catching prospect named Bill Dickey, whom he would cultivate and then sell to the Cardinals. This was when intervention from the unknown took place: Harper's car blew a tire.

While Harper was being delayed on the back roads of Arkansas, Lena Blackburne, manager of the Little Rock club was also heading for Hot Springs with a contract for Dickey. Thanks to Harper's bit of perforated rubber, Blackburne got there first, signed the eighteen-year-old boy, and thus applied a fateful spin to baseball history in both St. Louis and New York.

To many people, Bill Dickey was and remains baseball's ultimate catcher, a player without flaw. Defensively, he was impeccable; he could throw,

pitchers swore by his judgment, and he could hit—.313 lifetime batting average, including in 1936 a .362 mark, highest ever for a catcher. And he was durable, sharing the major league record with Cincinnati's Johnny Bench of catching one hundred or more games for thirteen consecutive seasons (1929 through 1941).

Yankee ace Spud Chandler had this to say of his batterymate:

He'd always encourage you, and he seemed to know what to call for. I never questioned Bill but one time in a ball game. We were playing in New York, and I was pitching against Washington. Through the first seven innings I hadn't thrown anything but fastballs. As we went into the dugout at the bottom of the seventh, I said, "Bill, when are you gonna call for a curve ball?" Without looking at me, he said, "When they start hitting your fastball."

● *Putting on the gear at the Yankees' St. Petersburg spring training camp in the early 1930s.*

● *Carl Reynolds.*

He called for one curve in the eighth and one in the ninth. Then Detroit came in, and he called for but three curveballs in that game. I guess he saw that my fastball was running and sinking so good he'd stick with it. But I threw only five curveballs in two games and won them both easily. You didn't argue with Bill Dickey.

Soft-spoken and gentlemanly he surely was; always, in the words of longtime American League catcher Birdie Tebbetts, "cool and at his ease." But like any great athlete, a fire burned in Dickey, and one afternoon it roared uncharacteristically from its furnace. Burly Carl Reynolds, outfielder of the Washington Senators,

came sliding hard and high-spiked into the plate, knocking Dickey flat. When the dust had settled and both men got to their feet, Dickey, thinking Reynolds was coming at him, suddenly decked him with a right hand that broke Reynolds' jaw. It cost the Yankee catcher a $1,000 fine and a thirty-day suspension. Dickey was embarrassed and contrite.

"I had done a terrible thing," he said, "and fully deserved the punishment."

But Yankee manager Joe McCarthy later said, "Sure, Bill shouldn't have hit the fellow; but I can tell you, after that they were a bit more polite when sliding in on him."

Dickey was born in Bastrop, Louisiana, on June 6, 1907, but was raised in Kensett, Arkansas, where Missouri Pacific Railroad man John Dickey moved his wife and seven children. After grade school at Kensett, young William Malcolm entered high school at Searcy, four miles away, where his baseball abilities began drawing attention. From there it was on to Little Rock College. During his years of higher education, Dickey played some semipro ball for a team in Hot Springs, where he was scouted and then signed by the Little Rock club of the Southern Association.

Farmed out by Little Rock in 1926, Dickey played for the Muskogee, Oklahoma, team in the Western Association, batting .283 in sixty-one games before being brought up to Little Rock, where he got into twenty-one games and batted .391. In 1927, he was with the Jackson, Mississippi, team in the Cotton States League, batting .297 and beginning to attract a lot of attention with his all-around skills.

Because the Chicago White Sox had a working agreement with Little Rock, it was assumed in baseball circles that they would buy Dickey. What happened, however, is virtually a textbook example of why the White Sox won no pennants between 1919 and 1959 and the Yankees won many. Chicago decided to pass on Dickey, while Yankee scout Johnny Nee, who had been watching the young catcher, wired back to New York, "I will quit scouting if this boy does not make good." The Yankees accepted their scout's judgment and thus acquired the man who was to become "the father of Yankee catchers," putting a seal of excellence on that critical position that was to last for half a century, the lineage running on virtually unbroken from Dickey through Yogi Berra, Elston Howard, and Thurman Munson.

Under the terms of the deal, Dickey spent the 1928 season with Little Rock, not joining the Yankees until the end of the season.

After having a good, long look at his new catcher in spring training 1929, Yankee manager Miller Huggins said of Dickey, "He's my catcher." The youngster was an immediate success, catching 130 games in his rookie year, batting .324, and leading the league with ninety-five assists. "They saw he was a new man," Yankee teammate Earle Combs said, referring to Dickey and American League base-stealers, "and they figured they'd try him out. They tried, and they found out."

"He was a perfectionist," McCarthy said of Dickey. "When I took over the team in 1931, he was in his third season and, along with Mickey Cochrane, was recognized as one of the two top catchers in the game. But Bill was still working like the devil to improve himself. He said you could never be good enough on digging out low pitches and you'd see him working on that in spring training. He taught himself to be quicker behind the plate. He said the trick was always to be aware of your body balance; that way you would always be ready for what might happen. He was just a pleasure to have on the club, as a man and as a player."

But not even the reserved, self-effacing Dickey was immune from the commission of clubhouse pranks. One day, a raw egg found its way into the Yankee clubhouse. Now, a raw egg in the hands of a baseball player has little chance of being boiled, poached, or scrambled, especially when the hands belong to Tony Lazzeri, slugging second baseman and unabashed man of mischief.

Lazzeri flipped the egg across the room to Dickey and then pointed to a pair of nearby spiked shoes. The shoes belonged to Babe Ruth. Lazzeri jabbed an insistent finger toward them; Dickey smiled, shrugged, and slipped the egg inside one of them. Then everyone sat back and waited.

● *Babe Ruth. Dickey had him walking on egg-shells.*

Ruth, as he often was, was late. When finally the great man came roaring in, be began hastily getting ready for the game. But all of his hurried movements came to an abrupt halt when he pushed his foot into the loaded spike and then slowly pulled it back dripping with the ripe insides of a broken egg.

The furious Ruth looked around and immediately spotted the guilt on Dickey's face (Bill was so unused to involvement in capers that he had never perfected an innocent expression). Ruth was angry, and even though Dickey was by that time a four-year veteran, a regular, a star, Babe Ruth was still Babe Ruth, and the frown of a monarch was enough to paralyze even a Bill Dickey.

But then Ruth, who had pulled many a practical joke in his day, suddenly erupted with laughter, and went about changing his sanitary understocking.

"Babe Ruth was a great guy in more ways than one," Dickey said years later, still grateful for the big man's raucous sense of humor.

Lou Gehrig, crown prince to the sovereign Ruth, was Dickey's roommate and closest friend on the club. Dickey, in fact, seems to have been the only teammate the mighty first baseman was ever genuinely close to (Dickey was the only Yankee player invited to Gehrig's wedding to Eleanor Twitchell on September 29, 1933).

Through his first six full seasons, Dickey's low batting average was .310 in 1932, a year he helped the Yankees pave the Cubs in four straight in the World Series with a .438 average. In 1935, he slipped to .279, but came roaring back a year later with his .362 average, still the all-time high for a catcher. A year later, in 1937, he put together his most explosive power season, hitting twenty-nine home runs and driving in 133 runs, while batting .332. And just for good measure, he led American League catchers in putouts, assists, and fielding percentage (one of six times he led in the last category).

By the late 1930s, Dickey had become one of the two choices for greatest catcher of all time, the other being Mickey Cochrane. Cochrane's adherents extolled their man's higher batting averages (a .320 lifetime, though Dickey at the end of the 1939 season had the same figure), running speed, and bruising competitiveness. Dickey's supporters claimed superiority in throwing, defensive finesse, and power (there was no argument about the latter). It came down to a coin-toss. When asked which of the two he would prefer, one veteran player put it perhaps best: "It would depend on who else you had on the team and what kind of club it was. Mickey might fit in better here, Bill there. But whichever one you had, you had a winner."

Through the 1941 season, Dickey completed his record thirteen straight years of catching one hundred or more games per season, fulfilling another requirement for greatness at the position—durability. Bill's constant readiness to play

● *Arndt Jorgens, who for ten years had one of baseball's most thankless jobs—backup catcher to Bill Dickey.*

● *Dickey at work during the 1941 World Series against the Brooklyn Dodgers. It's the 7th inning of Game 1 and Brooklyn's Cookie Lavagetto is sliding home safely. The umpire is Bill Mc-Gowan; number 8 is Dixie Walker.*

virtually sedated the career of his backup man, Arndt Jorgens, who was with the Yankees from 1929 through 1939 and caught just 285 games.

"I always thought Jorgens was a pretty good catcher," McCarthy said. "But nobody could be sure, because Dickey was so good and was so durable the other guy seldom got a chance to play."

Dickey's average sputtered to .247 in 1940, which was a let-down year for the entire team. After four straight world championships the Yankees finished third. Dickey and the club both came

back, however, Bill reviving with averages of .284, .295, and .351 as the Yankees took three straight pennants in 1941, 1942, and 1943. By 1943, he was only catching half the club's games (though by this time Arndt Jorgens had retired and never did get his shot).

It was during the 1943 World Series against the St. Louis Cardinals, shortly before the thirty-six-year-old Dickey entered the United States Navy, that he had what he called "my greatest day in baseball."

The Yankees took a three-games-to-one advantage and were playing the fifth game in St. Louis. Ace pitchers Mort Cooper of the Cardinals

● *Yankee manager Joe McCarthy (center) and the heroes of New York's Game 5 world championship victory over the Cardinals in the 1943 World Series. Bill Dickey (left) hit the two-run home run that enabled Spud Chandler to hurl a 2–0 shutout.*

and Spud Chandler of the Yankees were in a lock-step duel that carried a scoreless game into the top of the sixth inning. Then, with one man on, Dickey hit one "good, but not hard." Well, it was hit good enough and hard enough to carry out to the right-field pavilion in old Sportman's Park. It gave the Yankees a 2–0 lead, a score that stood until the end of the game. Dickey said that the full impact of the home run didn't sink in until he was lying in bed that night and suddenly began glowing with the thought that "I'd won the game and the Series with one blow and we were champions again."

Dickey spent the next two years in the Navy, then returned for his final year in 1946. He caught infrequently, getting into just fifty-four games. In late May, longtime skipper Joe McCarthy unexpectedly resigned and Dickey was appointed to replace him. It was a job the veteran catcher had not sought, nor did he particularly enjoy it.

It was a disappointing year for the Yankees—the Red Sox ran off with an easy pennant—and on September 12 Dickey was relieved of the manager's job.

Dickey, who was elected to the Hall of Fame in 1954, later scouted and coached for his old club; but the most valuable post-career contribution he made to the Yankees was the wise and patient coaching he gave to the unlikely looking young man who soon became his successor, Yogi Berra, who was to give the team another fifteen years of greatness behind the plate.

"Bill," the appreciative Berra said memorably, "is learning me his experience."

● *The perfect catcher.*

Ernie Lombardi with Brooklyn in 1931.

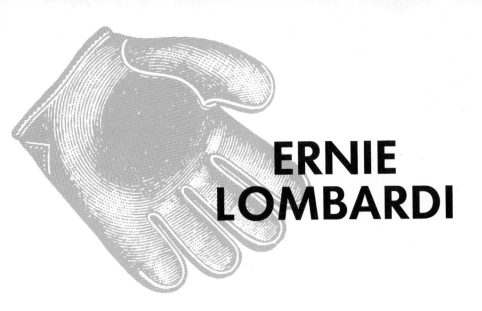

ERNIE
LOMBARDI

The legend of Ernie Lombardi was summed up by an old teammate, who said, "If Ernie Lombardi had possessed even average speed afoot he might have hit .400." Therein lies most of what baseball cares to remember about Cincinnati's hard-hitting catcher of the 1930s—blistering line drives and leaden feet.

Lombardi was big (6'3", 230 pounds), extremely strong, with hands the size of coffee tables. He was a right-handed hitter who, using a curious interlocking finger grip on the bat handle, could hit a ball with extraordinary might. Billy Herman, stellar second baseman of the Chicago Cubs in Lombardi's time, said of Ernie, "If Lombardi played on an artificial surface, he might have killed somebody with one of his shots; that's how hard he hit a ball. He could hit a ball as hard as anybody I ever saw, and that includes Babe Ruth." New York Giant ace Carl Hubbell, who stood just 60 feet away from Lombardi's perilously sudden line drives, said, "Lom was the only man I ever was afraid would hit one back at me and kill me."

What saved National League third basemen and shortstops from possible decapitation was Lombardi's laboring way down the baseline, which was so ponderously slow it enabled the left side to play him back almost to the rim of the outfield grass, from where they were able to pick up Ernie's torpedo shots (which were already through a normal infield alignment) and throw him out.

"Some of his groundouts to the left side," teammate Paul Derringer said of Ernie, "were so deep they were almost outfield assists."

Making Ernie even more of a menace to the opposing infield was the fact that he generally did not elevate the ball—despite his great power, he never hit more than twenty home runs in a season—but rather hit, according to Hubbell, "screamers that began to sink almost as soon as he tagged them."

Lombardi's tortoiselike pace in spiked shoes was as storied as the blisters his line shots raised on the summer air. He wasn't slow, went one line, it was just that he ran so long in one place. In seventeen big league seasons

● *"A quiet man, soft-spoken, shy, with the strength of a giant."*

Lombardi was born in Oakland, California, on April 6, 1908. Given his size, he was a catcher from day one, on the sandlots and in pro ball. He broke into a few games as an eighteen-year-old with Oakland in 1926, then split the following season between his hometown club and Ogden, Utah, in the Utah-Idaho League. Then followed three years behind the plate for Oakland, during which he compiled averages of .377, .366, and .370. Those robust marks finally outweighed the big leagues' prejudice against him—his lack of speed. In 1931 he was acquired by the Brooklyn Dodgers.

Paul Richards, who was with the Dodgers when Ernie reported that spring remembered the rookie very well.

> He reported with a little cap on and a satchel about the size of one a doctor would carry. The ballplayers put together some money to buy him a hat. Everybody liked him. The first game he caught he was catching Dazzy Vance. Somebody swung at a ball and Lombardi ducked and the ball hit him on top of the head and bounced all the way back to the bench. A blow like that would have knocked out an ordinary man, but Lombardi just crouched down and gave another sign, just as if nothing had happened. I've seen him catch hard-throwing pitchers with his bare hand and just toss the ball back.

Ernie caught fifty games in his rookie year and batted .297. His emergence made the Dodgers catcher-rich—they also had young Al Lopez, a brilliant defensive catcher with an adequate bat. So that winter, Lombardi was traded to Cincinnati and there he settled in and began pursuing the career that would eventually lead to his (somewhat belated, some people thought) election to the Hall of Fame in 1986.

Ernie was a solid man behind the plate, though defensively not on par with his three great contemporaries, Hartnett, Cochrane, and Dickey.

he stole eight bases, and once when he beat out a bunt against the Giants at the Polo Grounds, the New York papers recorded the event in back-page headlines.

He was a quiet man, soft-spoken, shy, with the strength of a giant. Along with his enormous hands, his most prominent physical feature was his nose, which was the size of a knocker on a castle door. This cost him the nickname "Schnozz." Schnozz Lombardi, who won a batting crown in 1938 (.342) and another one in 1942 (.330), and who was the National League's Most Valuable Player in 1938. The only other catcher ever to win a batting crown was Cincinnati's Bubbles Hargrave in 1926.

● *(Left to right) Bucky Walters, Lombardi, manager Bill McKechnie, and Paul Derringer.*

"He lacked that quickness behind the plate," Derringer said.

But he was a smart catcher, with a strong arm; and he had another thing that you can't measure. You know, pitchers can get easily riled up on the mound; it doesn't take much, an error, a bad call by the umpire. So Ernie would come out there, oh so slow, and so big, with that peaceful personality, drop the ball in your glove, give you a soft word or two and then turn and walk back. You just couldn't help smiling and you'd forget your problem. The guy was all heart and soul.

Lombardi began entertaining Cincinnati fans with his hitting and kept them entertained for a decade. He played ten years for the Reds and batted over .300 seven times; from 1935 through 1938 (when he won his first batting title) his averages were .343, .333, .334, and .342. With his batting honors and MVP Award, 1938 was Ernie's banner season, for he was also the man behind the plate that June in both of Johnny Vander Meer's consecutive no-hitters.

With Lombardi guiding Cincinnati pitching aces Derringer and Bucky Walters to fifty-two victories in 1939 ("And don't ever underestimate that big guy behind the plate," Walters said), the Reds won the first of two consecutive pennants.

The 1939 Series, however, ended on the low note of Ernie's career, though through no fault of his own. The Reds were up against the New York Yankees, and in those years Yankee opponents were the surest terminal patients in baseball. The New Yorkers had won four straight pennants and were about to methodically dispatch the Reds with minimum effort for a fourth straight world championship.

The closest the Reds came to a victory was in Game 4, which was a 4–4 tie after nine innings. In the top of the tenth, the Yankees put Frank Crosetti on third and Charlie Keller on first with one out. Joe DiMaggio then singled to right, scoring Crosetti, and when the ball was boxed around in the field, Keller also headed for the plate. Baserunner and peg arrived almost simultaneously and the burly Keller, charging at top speed, crashed into Lombardi, stunning him. The ball rolled a few feet from Ernie, and DiMaggio, ever alert, saw this and raced home and scored, crossing the plate as the stunned Lombardi lay on the ground with the ball a few feet away.

● *The big men behind the plate in the National League in the 1930s. Ernie Lombardi (left) and Gabby Hartnett.*

Stuck with a dishwater–dull Series, the writers seized on the image of Cincinnati's big catcher knocked senseless on the ground with baserunners whizzing past him, dubbed it "Lombardi's swoon," and left Ernie a victim of journalistic overkill.

"They made that the big story of the Series," Walters said. "But it was a big story about nothing, because DiMaggio's run didn't matter. They beat us 7–4."

Lombardi batted .319 in 1940, second best in the league, and helped the Reds to another pennant. But this time there was no World Series story for Ernie; a foot injury held the big man to just three at bats as the Reds won in seven games.

When Ernie dipped to a .264 average in 1941, the Reds traded him to the Boston Braves. The big man attributed the surprise trade to what was probably the only loose-lipped comment he ever made. Ernie had a salary dispute with Cincinnati general manager Warren Giles after his big 1938 season and in his pique made the mistake of publicly referring to Giles as an "old goat."

"I knew the first bad season I had Giles would get even with me," Lombardi said, and so it was off to Boston. But then Ernie got even with Giles. Whipping himself into the best shape of his life, he went on to win his second batting title with a .330 average.

In the spring of 1943, Ernie was traded to the New York Giants, with whom he finished his career in 1947. An occasional player in his seventeenth and final big league season, Ernie contributed four home runs to the 221 the Giants struck that year, which established a new major league record (since broken).

Lombardi, who died on September 26, 1977, left behind a .306 lifetime average, along with the legends of his terrifying line drives and his slower-than-slow feet. He also left behind a reputation for kindness, which was recalled by Tommy Holmes, a Boston teammate in 1942:

> I remember one time, we got on the train to take our first western trip of the year. We had a few rookies on the team and in those days they weren't making much money, maybe six hundred a month. They were pretty excited about making their first western trip. Well, Lombardi—bless him, I'll always remember him for this—went around to all the kids and said, "Hey, kid, got enough money?" And without waiting for an answer he'd push a twenty on them. Just wanted to make sure they had a few extra, to tip porters and waitresses, or buy themselves a beer, and so on. He wanted them to be able to feel like big leaguers. That was the kind of guy Ernie Lombardi was.

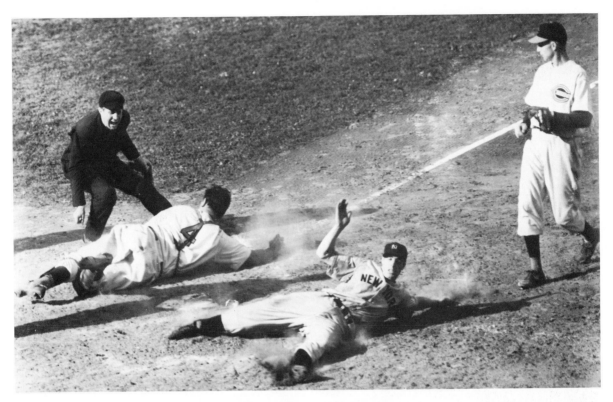

● *The ill-named "Lombardi swoon" in the tenth inning of the fourth and final game of the 1939 World Series. Ernie lies stunned as Joe Di-Maggio slides across the plate. Pitcher Bucky Walters is at the right and the umpire is Babe Pinelli.*

● *Lombardi with the New York Giants in 1947, his final year in the big leagues.*

. . .

Members of the Negro League Pittsburgh Crawfords
in 1932. (Left to right) Manager Oscar Charleston,
Rap Dixon, Josh Gibson, Judy Johnson, and Jud Wilson.

JOSH GIBSON

He did not play in the major leagues, so we lack a set of verifying statistics; but he did play for a long time, with and against and in front of a lot of reliable witnesses, and according to these, Josh Gibson was indeed a prince among sluggers and a king among catchers.

It is easy to issue accolades for those whom society dealt unjustly with, and gracious to believe them. In Gibson's case, however, not only has the legend persisted for so long, but there is so much of it, consistently, from so many people.

Gibson was, of course, one of the black players who never made it across the frontier finally traversed by Jackie Robinson. Josh was thirty-five years old when Robinson became the first black to play in the major leagues. Even though Gibson was one of the two most famous players in the Negro leagues—pitcher Satchel Paige was the other—he never received consideration from Brooklyn's Branch Rickey when the move to break the color barrier was being plotted. It wasn't just his age that militated against Gibson, for Josh was simply not the man Rickey was looking for; in addition to talent, "baseball's Abraham Lincoln" wanted a man of im-

peccable character to take on what would be the most difficult and important assignment in the history of professional sports. Josh had simply been around too long, and, almost unavoidably, it seemed, run up a rap sheet of peccadilloes that Rickey felt wouldn't do.

"For sheer talent alone," Rickey once confided to one of his assistants, "Gibson would have been the obvious choice. You know how I feel about Roy Campanella; but whatever Roy can do, Josh could do better."

Rickey's appraisal was shared by Campanella, who had for years played against Gibson in the Negro leagues.

"I couldn't carry his bat or glove," Roy said of Gibson. "The stories of his five-hundred-foot home runs are all true, because I saw them. And he was one of those sluggers that seldom struck out. You couldn't fool him, he was too quick with the bat. And he could do it all behind the plate, including throw."

Gibson was born in Buena Vista, Georgia, on December 21, 1911. He broke into

● *Josh Gibson. "I couldn't carry his bat or glove,"*
Roy Campanella said of him.

professional ball with the Homestead Grays in
1930 and immediately startled everyone with his
long-distance hitting. In those years there were
post-season barnstorming tours between major
league and black all-star teams. One year, Dizzy
Dean, then at the height of his considerable talents, was on the tour.

"Nobody hit me like Gibson did," Dean said.
"Some of our guys who played in the American
League said he hit the ball harder and further
than Jimmie Foxx. Well, all I know is that he hit
the ball harder and further off of me than anybody else ever did, before or after."

First baseman Buck Leonard, who teamed
with Gibson on the Grays to give the team an
awesome one-two punch (Leonard was known
as "The black Lou Gehrig"), recalled a shot
Gibson launched one day in Monessen, Pennsylvania. The blast animated the curiosity of the
town's mayor to the extent that he had the dis-
tance measured. "They determined," Leonard
said, "that the ball had traveled 575 feet from
home plate. But nobody on our team was ex-
cited, because we'd seen Josh do that before."

James (Cool Papa) Bell, an outfielder with the
Grays, and who was one of a handful of Negro
League stars voted into the Hall of Fame at Cooperstown, described Gibson as "the most powerful hitter" he had ever seen, white or black.
"Never swung hard at the ball either," Bell said.
"Just a short swing. Never swung all the way
around. Ruth used to hit them *high*. Not Gibson.
He hit them *straight*. Line drives, but they kept
going. His power was to center field, right over
the pitcher's head."

Walter Johnson, who saw Gibson play in the
1930s, said, "There is a catcher that any big
league club would like to buy for $200,000. His
name is Gibson. He can do everything. He hits
the ball a mile, he catches so easily he might as
well be in a rocking chair, throws like a bullet. Bill
Dickey isn't as good a catcher. Too bad this
Gibson is a colored fellow."

It was too bad for too long, for Gibson and
Bell and Leonard and Paige and so many others.
They were doomed to ply their trade on the obscure rimlands of America's game, following the
sun to make a living on the diamonds of North
and South America, Latin America, the Caribbean, creating their own perishable legends,
beyond the realm of record books and instant
historians. Accepting Josh Gibson as one of the
game's towering catchers is more than an act of
faith, for of all the many blacks who played
before Jackie Robinson, he was universally acknowledged as the best.

If not for Rickey and Robinson and the social revolution they fostered, then who knows for how long black players would have been barred from organized ball? Willie Mays, Hank Aaron, Ernie Banks, and other young black players began their careers in the Negro League, and if they had been denied the opportunity to play major league ball, then we would be hearing stories about their playing prowess, and probably with skepticism. If someone had said that Mays was as good as Joe DiMaggio or that Aaron might have broken Ruth's all-time home run record, the doubters would have been heard in full chorus.

The great unrecorded star Josh Gibson died early, only thirty-five years old, on January 20, 1947. Robinson had just completed his first year in organized ball and was obviously headed for the major leagues. Gibson died suddenly. They said it was a stroke. One old friend said that maybe a broken heart had had something to do with it.

"He saw that things were going to change," the friend said. "He was happy for that. But he knew that he had been born too soon."

● *James (Cool Papa) Bell.*

Yogi Berra in 1947.

YOGI BERRA

It was spring training 1947. The New York Yankees weren't quite sure what they had in this fellow. One writer, whose first glimpse of Lawrence Peter Berra was when the young man was still in the Navy, said, "If you think he doesn't look like a ballplayer in a baseball uniform, you should have seen him trying to look like a sailor in a sailor suit."

But young Berra wasn't trying to be anything or look like anything that he was not; all he wanted to be was himself, and that would prove to be considerably more than enough—one of baseball's most formidable hitters and brilliant catchers, a World Series star, a Hall of Famer, a pennant-winning manager, an American folk hero, and inadvertant contributor to the national repository of wisdom ("It ain't over 'til it's over.").

A school dropout at fifteen, Berra's lack of formal education probably deepened what seemed to be a natural shyness and contributed to the malaprops that made him more widely quoted than most poets. (Of Yankee Stadium's left field, made treacherous by the late afternoon sun: "It gets late early out there." Of a player vehemently disputing an umpire's call: "He was frosting at the mouth.") But in the world of

baseball, where precision of expression was not a prerequisite, the word on Berra was, "Listen to what he says, not how he says it."

He was born in St. Louis, on May 12, 1925, and grew up in an Italian neighborhood known as The Hill. He played American Legion ball; one of his teammates and also close friend was Joe Garagiola, who would find stardom behind the microphone after pursuing a big league career of modest achievement.

The priceless nickname was hung on Berra as a youngster. Some of Larry's friends had seen in a movie a Hindu fakir sitting in the motionless, arms-and-legs-folded posture of yoga. It reminded the boys of their friend, who often sat expressionless with folded arms between innings of a ball game. "Yoga" became "Yogi" and thus was minted a sports I.D. to rank with "Babe" and "Dizzy."

There were two big league clubs in St. Louis at the time: the Cardinals and the Browns. The Cardinals signed Garagiola for a $500 bonus and

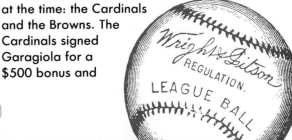

● *World Series victory celebrations were common in Berra's Yankee heydays. Here are four members of the 1952 world champs: Berra (top left) and Mickey Mantle, and (bottom left) pitchers Allie Reynolds and Vic Raschi.*

would have signed Berra, too, but the Cardinals general manager, Branch Rickey, was planning to move east and run the Brooklyn Dodgers and figured he would put Berra under a peach basket for awhile and then sign him to a Dodger contract. But for once the manipulative Rickey's plans went awry; the Yankees signed Berra, giving him a $500 bonus and a $90-a-month contract with the Norfolk, Virginia, club of the Piedmont League. This was in 1943.

The eighteen-year-old Berra caught 111 games for Norfolk in 1943, batted .253, hit seven home runs, and then joined the Navy. The youngster spent D-Day, June 6, 1944, on a landing craft that was sending and receiving messages several hundred yards offshore. He emerged unscathed, looking ahead to peacetime and the resumption of his career.

That career picked up again in 1946, with the Yankees' top farm club at Newark, in the International League. A .314 season earned him a trip to Yankee Stadium at the tail-end of the schedule. In seven games he hit two home runs and batted .364. The shy, pleasant rookie's homely appearance brought out the cruel humor of the locker room, but Berra just smiled and ignored the foolish banter.

"They stopped laughing when they saw him hit," said pitcher Vic Raschi, also joining the club at the time. "He had this smooth, easy swing, and the ball just jumped off his bat. And he always hit it. He had one of the best batting eyes I've ever seen." (Raschi was correct; in only three seasons of his long career did the power-hitting Berra strike out as many as thirty times.)

In time, Berra would become one of the most highly respected catchers in baseball, gaining praise for his defensive qualities and the acumen he showed in calling a game. But in the beginning, it was his hitting that kept him employed with the Yankees.

"He didn't seem to know a damn thing about catching when he first came up," said Bucky Harris, Yankee manager in 1947 and 1948.

> He called for too many fast balls, especially with a man on first, so he would have a better shot on an attempted steal. His arm was strong but he had the tendency to make high throws to second. His mechanics were all wrong. But he had a lot of natural ability, he showed a willingness to work hard and improve himself, and he could hit. Boy, could he hit.

In 1947, his first full year in the majors, Berra got into eighty-three games, fifty-one of them behind the plate and the rest in left field. He

● *"He always hit it," Vic Raschi said. Yogi is holding "it."*

batted .280 and hit eleven home runs. A year later, he got into 125 games, again dividing his time between catching and left field. This time he batted .305, parked fourteen home runs and drove in ninety-eight runs. The young man was now in the anteroom of stardom and everyone knew it. Yankee general manager George Weiss had the fact confirmed for him that winter.

"Every other phone call I received after the season," Weiss said, "was someone asking if Berra was available and what we wanted for him. That tells you everything you want to know about a player."

The Yankees had no intention of trading Berra, especially after Casey Stengel became manager in 1949. Along with Berra's obvious talents, Stengel also appreciated his intangibles: Yogi's keen baseball instincts, his quiet but colorful personality, the relaxing influence he had on his teammates. It was Stengel who brought Bill

Dickey to the Yankees' spring camp in 1949 to, as Berra was to put it, "learn me his experience." And Yogi indeed became the vessel into which Dickey poured all of the skills, tricks, and techniques that had been acquired during many years behind the plate.

"They say he's not the smartest fella in the world," Stengel said of Dickey's protégé, "but all I know is that you don't have to tell him something more than once before he knows it. I don't know how smart Mr. Berra is, but I do know that he's not dumb." And that *Mister* Berra was not one of Stengel's chance locutions. Casey was not always quick to laud his players, but in Berra he soon came to realize that he had a man who made managing a whole lot easier, and the skipper appreciated it. And for the benefit of his pitchers, some of whom were still making wisecracks about Berra's intellect, Stengel said, "My pitchers had better realize that Mr. Berra is the best friend they have on this ball club."

Berra soon became the Yankees' mooring post behind the plate, averaging around 140 games a season, leading American League catchers for a major league record eight consecutive years in games caught (1950–1957). From July 28, 1957, through May 10, 1959, Berra set records by playing in 148 consecutive games and accepting 950 chances without committing an error.

Berra's subtle skills under the bat were overshadowed by his hitting. In 1950 he batted a career high .322, hit twenty-eight home runs and drove in 124 runs. His all-around play earned him third spot in the MVP voting, but in 1951 and again in 1954 and 1955 he won the coveted award, while placing second in 1953 and 1956.

Like his great predecessor Dickey, who had been overshadowed by Ruth, Gehrig, and DiMaggio, Berra also found long and glamorous shadows around him. First it was DiMaggio's, whose shadow grew longer in its twilight, and then Mickey Mantle's, with all its bristling,

● *Berra with hard-hitting teammates Roger Maris (left) and Mickey Mantle.*

● *Some top-drawer talent getting together during spring training in the early 1960s. (Left to right) Mickey Mantle, Stan Musial, Yogi Berra, and Ken Boyer, who had ten MVP Awards among them. The man sitting is Yogi's boyhood chum Joe Garagiola.*

"My pitchers had better realize that Mr. Berra is the best friend they have on this ball club"—Casey Stengel.

breathtaking talent. Nevertheless, the big man on a host of Yankee pennant winners in the 1950s was Berra, the team RBI leader for seven straight years (1949–1955).

Yogi was a winner, playing in a record fourteen World Series (out of seventeen full seasons), enabling him to set many all-time Series records, including those for games (75), at bats (259), and hits (71). In the 1956 Series against Brooklyn, he batted .360 and drove in ten runs in seven games, and helped make history by hanging out the signals for Don Larsen's perfect game in Game 6.

Berra was particularly dangerous in pressure situations. "I remember one time," said former White Sox and Orioles manager Paul Richards,

A New York sportswriter came into our clubhouse moaning about Berra not hitting—Yogi was around .270 or so at the time. I told him to go back to the hotel tonight and check back through his scorebook and see what Berra's hitting from the seventh inning on. The guy showed up the next day with a sheepish look on his face and said, "Well, I give up. From the seventh inning on he's hitting .430."

Another element in the legend of Yogi Berra was his reputation for "bad-ball" hitting. He was known to swing at—and hit—pitches that were sailing over his head or burrowing around his ankles. But again there is another opinion from on high—from Warren Spahn, whose 363 major league victories are the most ever by a left-hander. The Spahn report comes via right-hander Gene Conley, Spahn's teammate on the Milwaukee Braves.

Spahn pitched to Yogi quite a bit over the years, and he used to deflate the legend about Berra being a bad-ball hitter. "He guesses with you," Spahn said. "That's what he does." So if a guy is guessing on a pitch and he gets it, then it doesn't matter if he's hitting at a bad ball, because he's ready for that pitch, he's already timed it. I remember scouting reports we had on Yogi in the 1957 World Series. They said he'd swing at anything, a ball in the dirt, or over his head, or whatever, and that to be careful when you got ahead of him, because he'd go after the bad pitch. But Spahn said, "I don't want to listen to that story." He said that in a tight spot, when Berra was really bearing down at the plate, he wouldn't offer at pitches that were just off the corner, that you had to throw him strikes. I believe Spahn was right about Yogi being a guess hitter.

By 1958, Berra was thirty-three years old and his years of catching most of his team's games was beginning to run its toll. Also, the club

• • •

Roy Campanella.

ROY CAMPANELLA

His was a career that began too late and ended too early. Roy Campanella was thirty-six years old when he suffered the accident that ended his baseball career and nearly took his life. The accident occurred as Campanella was driving to his Long Island home on the cold night of January 28, 1958. His car failed to negotiate a slick surface, spun off the road, struck a telephone pole and overturned, hurling Campanella about with wrenching violence. His injuries included fractures and dislocations of neckline vertebrae that left him paralyzed from the chest down, doomed to spend the rest of his life in a wheelchair.

The public at large and baseball fans in particular were heartsick over Campanella's tragedy, for not only was he one of the game's greatest catchers and a three-time Most Valuable Player, but the round-bodied, muscular Brooklyn Dodger star was as universally beloved for his jovial, good-natured disposition as he was admired for his superb playing skills.

Roy Campanella had followed the hard road through life and then on into the profession in which he was to excel. He was born on No-

vember 19, 1921, in Homestead, Pennsylvania, and raised in a section of North Philadelphia known as Nicetown.

Son of a black mother and Italian father, Roy was one of five children. The hard-working parents and cooperative children bound together to form a tight family unit. When he was nine years old the younger butterball-shaped Roy was earning some money by delivering newspapers, cutting grass, shining shoes, and helping an older brother who had a milk delivery route.

And of course there was baseball. The talent was there from the start and Campanella's was of a dimension that inevitably triggers all of the impulses and desires that motivate the great player. The dream is always wide and radiant, and when you have the kind of ability that this boy did, it becomes intense.

But for Roy Campanella and for all black youngsters of the time, the dream was surrounded by a lacing of barbed wire. Professional baseball existed beyond the moat of a color barrier. The barrier was unofficial and undeclared, an unwritten law, the kind that is hard to break because supposedly it does not exist.

There was, however, a Negro National League, a conglomeration of professional teams that boasted the finest black talent in the land. When he was just fifteen years old, Campanella was good enough to be signed by one of these clubs, the Baltimore Elite Giants.

For black players, this was the big leagues, but in life-style it was strictly the bushes, and worse. They traveled the country in buses that often doubled as rolling hotels. Management couldn't afford, or wouldn't spend, the money for a restful night's sleep, not that those hotels would have provided much rest or comfort, for most of the better ones would not register blacks. Nor were there restaurants, in certain parts of the country, that would serve them. And so they slept in their rattling buses and fed themselves as best they could as they followed the back-lane baseball trails of America. When the cold winds blew the summer game to sleep they followed the baseball sun to Mexico and Latin America and the Caribbean, and they kept playing and playing.

So Roy Campanella learned his trade and soon became as good at it as any man in the country. His catching skills were impressive, his throwing arm of eye-catching strength and accuracy; he ran well for a man of his girth, and he could bust a baseball a long way. All that stood between Campanella and the glamor and comforts of national recognition was a thrust of social progress.

Jackie Robinson is remembered today as the first black to sign a contract with organized baseball (in October 1945) and as the first to play in the big leagues (with Brooklyn in 1947). Spending the 1946 season with Montreal, then a Triple-A club in the International League, Robinson drew considerable attention. But Jackie wasn't the only black player in the vanguard of Brooklyn president Branch Rickey's effort to surmount baseball's barricade of prejudice. That

● *Dodger manager Walter Alston (left) and Campanella in 1955.*

same 1946 season saw catcher Roy Campanella and pitcher Don Newcombe breaking in with Brooklyn's Nashua, New Hampshire, farm team in the Class B New England League. The manager was Walter Alston, later to manage the Dodgers in Brooklyn and Los Angeles for twenty-three years.

"Roy of course was better than a Class B player," Alston said.

> But he knew why he was there. He was part of Rickey's plan to begin integrating baseball. He even took a salary cut to get into pro ball. He was making around $500 a month in the Negro League, but only $185 at Nashua. But he never complained about that, because he knew he was helping to start something important. And anyway, I've never seen a more enthusiastic guy on a ball field, one who got more sheer joy out of playing.

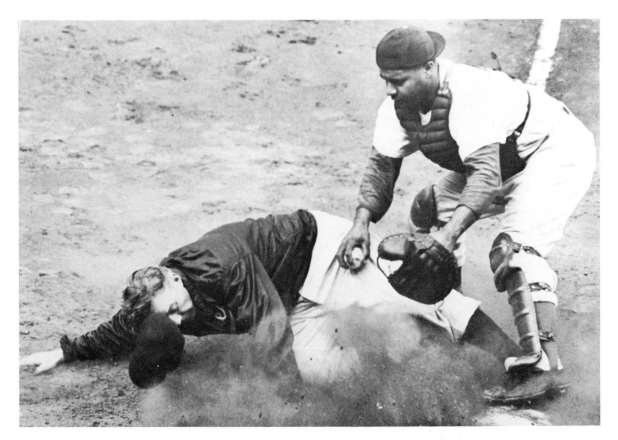

● *Campanella tagging out the Yankees' Eddie Lopat during the 1949 World Series.*

Campanella batted .290 and was voted the league's Most Valuable Player. In 1947, the year Robinson began bringing democracy to the major leagues, Roy played for Montreal and turned in another strong showing. He went home after the season with the expectation of being Brooklyn's starting catcher in 1948. Branch Rickey, however, had other ideas.

In the spring of 1948, Roy was told he would be starting the year with St. Paul of the American Association.

"But, Mr. Rickey," Roy said, "I've earned my shot with the Dodgers."

"No question," Rickey said. "But if I let you start catching for Brooklyn I won't be able to send you out."

"What's wrong with that?"

"Because," the melodramatic Rickey confided, "it is your mission to integrate the American Association. Right now, that is of paramount importance."

And so, muttering that he didn't want to be a pioneer, Campanella went to St. Paul. But not for long. After thirty-five games he had hit thirteen home runs and was batting .325, and it was no longer possible to keep him in the minor leagues. At the end of June he was called up to Brooklyn and took over the job he would hold for ten years.

With Campanella anchoring the team behind the plate, the Dodgers began a decade of dominance during which they won five pennants and

● *Key members of the great Dodger teams of the 1950s. (Left to right) Duke Snider, Gil Hodges, Jackie Robinson, Pee Wee Reese, and Roy Campanella.*

placed second three times. It was a team of predominantly right-handed power, so designed by Rickey to take advantage of Ebbets Field's neighborly fences in left and left-center. Along with Campanella were second baseman Robinson, shortstop Pee Wee Reese, first baseman Gil Hodges, the magic-gloved Billy Cox at third, and Carl Furillo and Duke Snider (the only lefty swinger in the lineup) in the outfield. Campanella

nurtured a pitching staff that included Newcombe, Carl Erskine, Clem Labine, and left-handers Johnny Podres and Preacher Roe, all of whom extolled their great catcher.

"Just seeing him back there made you a better pitcher," Podres said.

"He was something of the psychologist," Newcombe said. "He knew that sometimes if he got me mad I'd pitch better, so out he'd come in the middle of a game, this roly-poly guy, and give

● *Gil Hodges (left), Don Newcombe, and Campanella are smiling up another Dodger victory.*

me some needling. He knew when to do it and how." (In 1955 to 1956, Campy's calculated needling helped Newcombe to a combined 47–12 record.)

Alston, who always had a special fondness for Roy, said of him, "He was always doing something to help you win a game, whether it was digging out a low pitch, throwing out a baserunner, or hitting a home run. Sometimes you won simply because he was there—they wouldn't try to steal on him. That keeps a guy on base and helps keep your pitcher's concentration on the batter."

Playing on what was virtually an all-star team, Campanella had to share the headlines with the speed, power, or defensive splendor of one or another of his teammates. But when it came to selecting the most critically important man on this sterling roster, three times the sportswriters went to Campanella, voting him the league's most valuable player, in 1951, 1953, and 1955. In 1951, he batted a career high .325, hit thirty-three home runs, and drove in 108 runs. In 1953 he turned in one of the greatest offensive years any catcher ever had—.312 average, forty-one

home runs, and league-leading 142 runs batted in, and also led league catchers in fielding. In 1955, his MVP plaque was based on a .318 average, thirty-two home runs and 107 RBIs. (These were the years that led to his Hall of Fame election in 1969.)

"The way he was going," Alston said, "he might have won the MVP Award in 1954, too, but he suffered through the season with an injury to his left hand that was so severe it was partially paralyzed for awhile and eventually needed surgery."

In those years Campanella was running neck-and-neck on the same track as his only rival for catching supremacy, the Yankees' Yogi Berra, who also won three MVP Awards, in 1951, 1954, and 1955. Many a New York street corner, barber shop, and tavern was enlivened by learned discussions about the relative merits of Roy and Yogi. As far as is known, the only conclusion reached was that Yankee fans preferred Berra and Dodger fans Campanella.

Campanella was behind the plate for the seventh game of the 1955 World Series, when the Dodgers beat the Yankees to give Brooklyn the only world championship it would ever have. Johnny Podres, who pitched the masterful 2–0 shutout that gave the Dodgers the title, recalled the contribution of his catcher.

"That win was half Campy's," Podres said. "He never called a better game. He saw how my stuff was working and he seemed to know what the Yankee hitters were looking for. I don't think I shook him off but once or twice the whole game."

Injuries again impeded Campanella in 1956, when he batted just .219. In 1957, he batted .242 and caught one hundred games, his lowest amount since his rookie season. There was speculation that Brooklyn's great catcher was slowing down. Alston didn't think so.

"I would have started catching him a bit less," the skipper said. "You couldn't put him out there for 140 games anymore. But he was still the

● *By the looks of things, contact is imminent.*

● *Branch Rickey.*

soundest defensive catcher in baseball and all the things he did for your pitching staff were still invaluable. And remember where we played for the next few years,'' Alston added with a smile.

He was referring to the Los Angeles Coliseum, the lop-sided temporary home of the Dodgers when they moved to the west coast in 1958. While right and center fields called for cannon shots to get a ball over the fence, left field was just 251 feet down the line, spanning out to a mere 320 in left-center, the meager distances protected by a 42-foot screen.

''Campy would have had a picnic there for a few years,'' Alston said wistfully.

But there was that patch of slick road on Long Island on the cold night of January 28, 1958, the helpless horror of a skidding automobile, the crash, the impact, more than even the powerful body of Roy Campanella could withstand. The popular three-time MVP would never again swing a bat, at the Coliseum or anywhere else.

Cincinnati's rookie catcher Johnny Bench in 1968.

JOHNNY BENCH

It's one of baseball's nice stories; it tells of the grace of a monarch and the glow of a budding crown prince. In the spring of 1969, Ted Williams autographed a baseball to a twenty-one-year-old catcher this way: "To Johnny Bench, a Hall of Famer for sure."

You can be certain that this wasn't the customary message in the autographs Williams handed out to young ballplayers, but the greatest of hitters had already discerned what was becoming more and more evident to all: a unique new energy had been set loose in the universe of baseball.

Luke Sewell, a catcher who had excelled at the job for two decades, said,

It's the one position where you've got to put in time and get experience. I was catching in the American League when Cochrane and Dickey broke in, and believe me, as great as they were, they were both pretty rough-edged in the beginning. But this kid Bench—what is he, twenty-one years old?—he looks like he's been doing it for fifteen years.

That is exactly what Bench had been doing.

"I was planning on being a big league catcher since the first grade," Bench said. Well, so were a lot of kids, but along with his ambition this youngster had a brick-wall physique, a powerful arm, platter-sized hands, quickness, coordination, and a keen intelligence.

The boy's ambition had evolved out of his father's dream. With his own hopes of playing pro ball having been derailed by World War II, semipro catcher Ted Bench decided that his robust youngster would be the big leaguer in the family, and that the fastest route to glory was being a catcher, a position whose hardships and complexities were shunned by most youngsters.

Johnny Bench was born in Oklahoma City, on December 7, 1947, but grew up in Binger, some 50 miles west. Little more than a bump in the road, Binger had a population of 600 and a downtown of two blocks. But it was not without a boast, calling itself "The peanut capital of the world."

Along with peanuts, Binger also

● *Ted Williams, who knew talent when he saw it.*

produced cotton, wheat, sweet potatoes, alfalfa, not to mention Johnny Bench, who was first noticed by a Cincinnati scout while playing American Legion ball.

"What we heard about," a member of the Reds organization recalled, "was the size of the boy's hands—he reportedly could hold seven baseballs in one hand—the strength of his throwing arm and the maturity and professionalism he showed for a seventeen-year-old. Oh yes, in addition, he could also hit the ball a mile."

So, in June 1965, the Reds signed (for a bonus of about $10,000) the freshly minted high school graduate, put him on a plane, and flew him to Tampa, where he arrived at nine o'clock that night. From the airport the boy went straight to the ball park and was put right into the game,

catching the ninth inning. It was as if the Cincinnati organization couldn't wait to put Johnny Bench to work.

Baseball may be a boy's game, but it's a man's work. "I missed the years of growing up from seventeen to twenty-one," Bench said. "I passed over those years without living them. I missed all the things other guys live through— college fraternities, dances, dates, all those things. I had to go from being a boy to being a man overnight."

From Tampa in the Florida State League, Johnny went to Peninsula in the Carolina League (where he made so profound an impression the club retired his number after the season), and from there to Buffalo in the International League. By the end of the 1967 season Bench was catching for Cincinnati.

Bench had in abundance every tool the big league catcher needs, including self-confidence (an asset more important for a catcher than for any other player on the field). The young man called it "inner conceit," which he described as a "self-confidence kind of thing. It's knowing that you can do a certain thing, knowing within yourself you can meet any situation. A lot of young players lack that . . . . It's inner conceit that tells me, 'This guy can't steal off me if he doesn't get too big of a jump. And if he gets too far off base, I'll pick him off.' "

With the exuberance and impatience of youth, Johnny's "inner conceit" sometimes expressed itself. He broke his thumb in his first game at Buffalo and while nursing the injury attended some games at Crosley Field, then Cincinnati's home field. Given his special interests, the youngster, not yet nineteen years old, took a seat near the bullpen, where he could watch the pitchers warm up. One Cincinnati pitcher, Sammy Ellis, recalled Bench yelling down at them, "Hey, if any of you guys are catchers, you'd better remember me. I'm going to take one of your jobs." Two years later (in 1968) he was National League Rookie of the Year, beginning a league record

● *Ready for come what may.*

stretch of thirteen consecutive seasons of catching one hundred or more games, averaging 140 games for each of the first seven of those seasons. He had, in effect, taken all of their jobs.

A man with as much self-confidence as Bench had will sometimes allow himself to manifest a shade of arrogance. One night he was catching a slim left-hander named Jerry Arrigo. "He thought he had a fastball," Bench said. "He was pitching against a hitter I knew he couldn't possibly throw it by. I called for a curve and he shook it off, a curve again and he shook it off, a curve one more time and he shook it off. He finally threw a fastball outside." As much in contempt as with calculation, Bench reached out and caught the ball with his bare hand. Arrigo's eyes widened. "I didn't want to show him up," Johnny said, "but . . ." The point was made.

Bench caught 154 games in 1968, still the major league record for a rookie. It was not the best of times for a young slugger to be introducing himself, for 1968 was "The Year of the Pitcher," when National League pitchers posted a collective ERA of 2.99, lowest in half a century, and the league as a whole batted just .243. But Bench did just fine, batting .275, with fifteen home runs, an impressive forty doubles, and eighty-two RBIs.

Destined to be a long-distance-running star, Bench got his career off at an impressive sprint. In 1970, his third year in the majors, he was the league's Most Valuable Player, with league-leading figures in home runs (forty-five) and runs batted in (148). In 1972, he won the prestigious trophy again, once more leading in home runs (40) and runs batted in (125). He took a third RBI title in 1974 with 129.

Catchers weren't expected to hit like that (manager Sparky Anderson gave his star some "rest" time, playing him in the outfield or at third base now and then), especially one with the high-voltage abilities of Bench.

"You can't expect catchers to hit as consistently as the rest of the players," said Luke Sewell. "You see, their hands are always getting banged up behind the plate. Sometimes your hands are aching so much it's painful just to grip the bat. A catcher can have twenty or thirty points knocked off his batting average just from bruised hands. People don't take account of that because those aren't considered serious injuries."

With Bench as the foundation man, the Reds began their run as "The Big Red Machine," when Cincinnati put together what many people consider the greatest team in National League history, winning six Western Division titles and four pennants from 1970 through 1979. The club was a mosaic of gleaming talent, a galaxy of all-stars and Most Valuable Players (Bench in 1970 and 1972, outfielder Pete Rose in 1973, second baseman Joe Morgan in 1975 and 1976, outfielder George Foster in 1977).

● *The stars of "The Big Red Machine." (Left to right) Tony Perez, Johnny Bench, Joe Morgan, and Pete Rose.*

● *Bench (right) posing with Dodger manager Tom Lasorda.*

The question of who was baseball's all-time catcher had for decades been comfortably narrowed to Dickey and Cochrane, but by the mid-1970s it had been expanded to include a new entry, Johnny Bench, who caught as well as they had, who threw better, who was more explosive at the plate (though his batting averages were markedly lower, a point that must be footnoted by the fact that in the era of Cochrane and Dickey batting averages were generally higher). The question, of course, could never be conclusively answered, but the very fact of its being posited was enough, for it shared baseball's most eminent debating heights: who was the better hitter, Babe Ruth or Ted Williams; the fastest pitcher, Walter Johnson or Bob Feller; the better center fielder, Willie Mays or Joe DiMaggio? And now, who was the greatest catcher, Dickey, Cochrane, or Bench? The debate was sufficient unto itself.

Of all Bench's talents, the one that most fascinated baseball people was his throwing, so ferociously strong that it set him apart from all other catchers. In the words of Baltimore Orioles executive Harry Dalton, "Every time Bench throws, everybody in baseball drools."

There was something special about a Bench peg to second base; like a Babe Ruth home run or a Nolan Ryan fastball, it was stamped with its own unique brand. According to one Cincinnati infielder, "That ball would come in at you a few feet off the ground and you'd be set to short-hop it. But it just kept sizzling at you on a line, and when it hit your glove it was like a rock coming in." (There are some baseball people who maintain that at 60 feet Bench could throw as hard, if not harder, than Ryan.)

"No matter how much you knew about his arm," one scout said,

> Somehow you never quite believed it until you found out for yourself. Now, in the 1976 World Series the Yankees knew damned well how Johnny Bench could throw. But in baseball, just like in any other sport, you've got hard-assed

● *The question had been, Dickey or Cochrane? Then along came Johnny Bench.*

> competitors and they want to be shown. Now, Bench knew that. Early in the first game, Mickey Rivers, the Yankees' fastest man, tries to steal second. Bench double-pumped and then threw him out easily. The double-pump was deliberate. Now the Yankees knew what they were up against. I think they ran on him only once for the rest of the Series. Intimidation, that's what Bench achieved in the first game.

Sizeable enough to begin with, Bench's reputation was further enhanced by some dramatic post-season hitting. In 1972, the Reds and Pirates engaged in the playoff for the National League pennant. Then a five-game affair, the series worked its way to a fifth and deciding

Sparky Anderson: "Don't embarrass any catcher by comparing him to Johnny Bench."

game. Going into the bottom of the ninth, the Pirates held a 3–2 lead. Leading off for the Reds, Bench hit a long, high-riding home run into the right-center field bleachers to tie the score. The Reds then scored another run and won the pennant. In the 1976 playoffs between the Reds and Phillies, Bench did the same thing, though this time the circumstances were not as stark for the Reds. Cincinnati had won the first two games but were trailing 6–4 in the bottom of the ninth of the third game. After George Foster led off with a home run, Bench followed with another, making it 6–6. The Reds then continued on, scoring another run and winning the pennant.

In the 1976 World Series, which the Reds swept in four, Bench made a gourmet feast of Yankee pitching, getting eight hits, batting .533, and sealing Cincinnati's 7–2 championship victory in Game 4 with two home runs and five runs batted in.

In 1980, after setting a league record by catching one hundred or more games for the thirteenth straight year, Bench was feeling the accumulated aches and pains of over 1,700 games under the bat, and he decided that he had had enough. He spent the last three years of his career, 1981 through 1983, playing third or first, then retired and awaited his Hall of Fame induction, which came in 1988 (fulfilling Ted Williams' prophecy).

It was after the sweep of the Yankees in 1976 that Cincinnati manager Sparky Anderson threw diplomacy to the winds and came right to the point. When asked to compare Bench and Yankee catcher Thurman Munson, Sparky said, "Don't embarrass any catcher by comparing him to Johnny Bench."

Carlton Fisk.

CARLTON FISK

Talk about home runs, in New England there isn't but one. They still talk about it up in that most singular corner of the country as though it had become one of those timeless legends that stand as hard as New Hampshire granite and as mysterious as moonlit Maine woods. This most famous missile fired in the city of Boston since the battle of Bunker Hill shot free with the awesome suddenness of a meteor, struck on the night of October 21, 1975, and was climax to what many people contend was the most stirring World Series game ever played. The electrifying blow not only brought victory to New England's darlings, the Boston Red Sox, but it was launched into the night-sky of the city of Revere and Adams and Lowell by one of the area's own, Carlton Fisk, born in Bellow's Falls, Vermont.

The occasion was momentous, and there humanizing it right down to the ingenuousness of sandlot level was Carlton Fisk, moving tentatively toward first base, watching the ball rising high toward Fenway Park's left-field wall; for a tense moment there was the uncertainty of fair or foul, with Fisk lifting and pushing both hands toward fair territory, to guide or persuade or en-

courage that ball to do the right thing. It did, and the gestures became almost as famous as the home run.

If you went to some celestial workshop and asked to have designed for you the ideal catcher, he would probably come out looking like Carlton Ernest Fisk. At 6'3" and some 200 pounds, the physique was just about right, with the man inside it tough and intelligent, motivated by a desire to win that is ever the eternal flame of every outstanding athlete.

As rough-ready as all the great catchers have been and will always be because they have to, Fisk could be as tough on his own pitchers as on the opposition.

"You knew yourself if you weren't bearing down as hard as you might," one Red Sox pitcher said, "and on those occasions you hated to see him marching out there at you." And come out Carlton Fisk would, stern as a headmaster, with that mask resting on his head, to point out in the crispest terms the pitcher's derelictions.

● *Carlton Fisk wigwagging directional signals to the famous home run he struck at Fenway Park on the night of October 21, 1975.*

bearing notwithstanding. He grew up on a small farm and later went to the University of New Hampshire on a basketball scholarship. A natural athlete, he hoped to play pro basketball, but at 6'3'' he was a bit small, and anyway in 1967 the Red Sox came around and signed him for a small bonus.

Fisk spent the 1967 season in military service, then began working his way toward Fenway Park. In 1968 he played at Waterloo, Iowa, in the Midwest League, batting .338. A year later he was closer to home, with Pittsfield, Massachusetts, in the Eastern League. Despite a .243 average the Red Sox brought him up for a quick initiation at the end of the season. After two more seasons honing his skills at Pawtucket and Louisville, he came to stay in 1972.

The impact Fisk made in Boston in 1972 was impressive in many ways. The twenty-four-year-old catcher batted .293 and hit twenty-two home runs, he tied for the league lead with nine triples (he remains the only catcher in American League history to lead in three baggers), led in putouts and assists, and became the first (and thus far only) unanimous choice for Rookie of the Year.

But there was more to the young man than the box score told. In the midst of a tightly contested pennant race (which Boston lost on the season's penultimate day) a Massachusetts paper quoted the rookie catcher on two of his teammates: "They are not lending inspiration to the team and their attitude is a big disappointment." The teammates were veterans Carl Yastrzemski and Reggie Smith. This was unusually candid, particularly coming from a rookie, a genus that by unwritten baseball law is supposed to be a mute presence. But this was no ordinary rookie, not by any trim or measure.

Leadership, that hallmark of great catchers, came naturally to Fisk. Playing with an intensity that seemed to contain shades of hauteur, he sometimes irritated opponents, and on occasions he would deliberately anger his own pitcher, on the premise that, "If I can get a pitcher mad enough, he'll want to throw the ball right through me. He can't do that. But he might get a couple of batters out trying."

Or sometimes, the pitcher said, "He would fire the ball back at you as hard as he could, and that would deliver the message. I don't know which I dreaded more, the conversation or the telegram. But either way, he was telling you something you ought to know."

Fisk was born on December 26, 1947, in Bellow's Falls but was raised across the state line in Charlestown, New Hampshire, a place that resembled Hollywood's idealization of small town New England, with its clean and homey main street, church spires, and outlying farms.

They called him "Pudge" as a boy—nicknames often come too early in life—and it stuck, his later stately athletic build and parade ground

● *He was no ordinary rookie.*

He played hard, engaging in a swing-out at home plate with the Yankees' Thurman Munson after a hard Munson slide, an episode that left the league's two star catchers in a state of sullen mutual hostility that ended only with Munson's death.

Injuries limited Fisk to fifty-two games in 1974, and a spring training mishap in 1975 kept him out of the lineup until June 23. This was the baseball year that had waiting for Fisk his culminating moment, the sixth game of the World Series. For his half season's work the big catcher batted .331, helping a powerful Red Sox team get into the October pageant against the Cincinnati Reds, one of baseball's all-time great teams.

Fisk's memorable home run was the crescendo blow of a game already replete with sparkle and drama. Trailing 6–3 in the bottom of the eighth, the Red Sox had tied the score on a three-run pinch-hit home run by Bernie Carbo. In the bottom of the ninth, the Reds survived a bases loaded, none out furnace. In the top of the eleventh, Dwight Evans' spectacular catch robbed the Reds' Joe Morgan of a two-run home run.

And so the game rolled on, with over one hundred million people riveted to television sets around the country, watching what was already a classic of baseball artistry. Extra innings in Fenway Park is like playing with live ammunition, the proximity of its left field wall becoming more and more ominous. The leadoff batter for Boston in the last of the twelfth was Fisk. The moment was primed, the glory was there. All a man had to do was . . .

It happened on right-hander Pat Darcy's second pitch. Taking his hard, fluid cut, Fisk hit the ball hard. Hard enough, far enough. But fair or foul? Between the crack of the bat and the ball's climb and descent, Fenway Park fell suddenly still. At home plate Fisk began gesticulating excitedly, trying to communicate with the night-borne baseball.

"The wind was carrying it toward the foul pole," he said later. "I was trying to push it fair."

He succeeded, for the ball struck the pole for a home run, giving the Red Sox a 7–6 victory in "the greatest World Series game ever played."

Boston lost the Series in Game 7, but Carlton Fisk's post-midnight home run remains as the affair's defining image.

In 1977, Fisk was the iron man, catching 151 games and putting together a potent offensive season with twenty-six home runs, 102 runs batted in, and a .315 batting average. A year later he caught 154 games and again hit well. By now he had established himself as one of baseball's top catchers and surely the best the Boston Red Sox had ever had; but after the 1980 season the club was to lose him.

● *From Red Sox to White Sox. Fisk in 1981.*

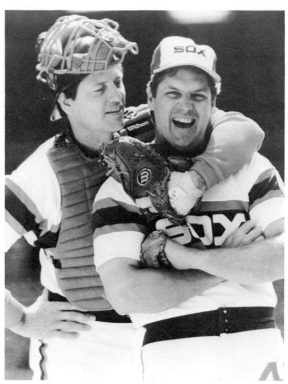

● *One of baseball's all-time classy batteries: Fisk (left) and Tom Seaver.*

Through a clerical error, Fisk's 1981 contract was mailed too late to him and a rules technicality was breached, entitling him to free agency. Suddenly finding himself on the open market in the midst of baseball's dollar hailstorm, Fisk sold himself to the Chicago White Sox and there settled in to begin "a second career."

"We signed him when he was thirty-three years old," a White Sox executive said in 1990. "Who knew he'd still be going strong ten years later?"

Strong, and at times stronger. After several years of steady hitting, Fisk erupted in 1985 with thirty-seven home runs, thirty-three of them as a catcher, setting a new league record for the position. In 1986, the club made a part-time outfielder of him and Fisk grumbled. He knew where his value lay (and so did the White Sox pitchers), and a year later he was back where he belonged, at the age of thirty-nine catching 122 games. In 1989 he batted .293 and added to his own record of games caught by an American League catcher, which now totaled 1,928. He also broke Yogi Berra's league home run record for the position with 315 (of a career total of 336) and set his sights on Johnny Bench's major league record for catchers of 327.

Already a twenty-year man at baseball's toughest and most demanding position, Fisk after the 1989 season signed a new two-year contract, making the boy from the tiny, picturesque New England town one of the game's all-time unstoppable forces.

● *All business: Carlton Fisk at work.*

• • •

Thurman Munson in 1970, the year he was voted the
American League's Rookie of the Year.

THURMAN MUNSON

To his teammates he had come to seem like the indestructible man. He had caught over one hundred games for nine straight years and was on his way to doing it for a tenth. He seemed to revel in the bruising activity behind the plate, fighting off foul tips and taking the jarring impact of baserunners. There was nothing stylish or graceful about him. If there was such a thing as a blue collar ballplayer, then he was it, with his dirty uniform, stocky body, and the measuring stare of an untipped cab driver.

Thurman Lee Munson was the fourth and last in the almost continuous line of gifted Yankee catchers that began with Bill Dickey in 1928, was carried ahead by Yogi Berra, and then Elston Howard, who caught his last game for the Yankees two years before Munson joined the club in 1969.

"He was ready for anything back there," Yankee manager Billy Martin said. "He knew there were times when he was going to get knocked on his ass, and when it happened you'd see him get up, put his mask back on and go back to work. I remember one of my coaches saying to me, after a real tough collision at the plate,

'You notice something? Thurman doesn't brush himself off.' " It was as though the earthen stains of the home plate area were to be worn as badges of honor.

"Thurman was one of the things you could always count on," Martin said. "That's why, when it happened, it was so unbelievable."

It happened on August 2, 1979. The Yankees had an off-day and Munson decided to take advantage of it and pay a visit to his Canton, Ohio, home. While there, he took up his recently purchased Cessna Citation to practice touch-and-go landings at the Akron-Canton airport. Still not a fully accomplished pilot, he was accompanied by an instructor and a friend. A miscalculation brought the plane down some 900 feet short of the runway and there was a crash. Fire erupted within the cabin, and though the passengers managed to survive, Munson suffered massive injuries on impact and was fatally pinned in his seat, where he died. He was thirty-two years old.

Munson was born in Akron, Ohio,

on June 7, 1947. He was raised in nearby Canton, later the site of the Football Hall of Fame, and though he had a football player's grit and ability to absorb punishment, baseball was the youngster's game. He did in fact play high school football and was good enough to attract scholarship offers in both sports, but chose the baseball scholarship offered by Kent State.

While starring at Kent State, Munson was scouted by ex-Yankee outfielder Gene Woodling, who was initially impressed by the young man's throwing arm and speed afoot. "I thought he had the tools to make it to the top," Woodling said later, "but frankly, his hitting surprised me. I never thought he would hit as well as he did."

Munson broke in with Binghamton in the Eastern League, in 1968, batting .301. After some fine tuning at Syracuse the next year, he was brought up to the Yankees. Munson had just eighty-six at bats for the Yankees in 1969, not enough to disqualify him as a Rookie of the Year candidate in 1970, when he in fact won the designation, handily, receiving every vote but one. The distinction was earned with a .302 batting average and rugged efficiency behind the plate, which included a league-high (for catchers) eighty assists, one of three times he led.

The new Yankee star hit only six home runs; his career high would be twenty in 1973, and in some years he failed to reach double figures in the long ball. Strong as he was, Munson was never considered a home run hitter, choosing instead to use the whole field. For a right-handed hitter in Yankee Stadium, a ball park with hostile distances in left and left-center, this was the smart way to go, and it was reflected in Munson's batting averages—he was a .300 hitter five times in his ten full seasons. From 1975 through 1977 he became the first big leaguer in more than a decade to link three straight seasons of .300 batting averages and one hundred runs batted in.

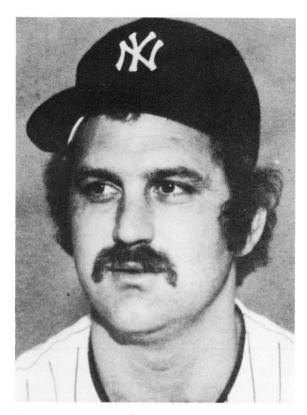

● *One sportswriter said of Munson, "He puts a kick in the team."*

When Munson joined the Yankees they were in the midst of their longest dry spell since the dead ball era. The Yankee dynasty—twenty-nine pennants from 1921 through 1965—had finally crumbled and come earthward with a thud. It would take another six years before the team began winning pennants again, in 1976 through 1978, but the first and most critical foundation block had been put in place with the arrival of Thurman Munson in 1970.

"He puts a kick in the team," one sportswriter said of Munson in the early 1970s. "The guy is tough and aggressive and fairly bristles with the desire to win. He's the kind of player you salivate to have on your side, but pardon me if I don't invite him to dinner."

The latter was a commentary on the Munson personality, or at least the side of it that was frequently turned to the press. Thurman was variously described as shy, insecure, hypersensitive, unfriendly, moody, suspicious, and downright nasty. One supposes that it all depended.

"He was basically a good guy," one teammate said (Munson was popular with his teammates, all of whom accepted his leadership, with one prominent exception, as we shall soon see). "But I've never seen a guy get so deeply into a game, and he'd still be in it after it was over, when the writers came around for post-game stories. He resented the intrusion and he was the kind of guy who let them know about it."

Munson could be, one writer said, ". . . boorish, rude, and, at times, outright offensive." Those writers willing to suspend judgment often found the sensitive man underneath. And sensitive he was, about his physique (teammates called him "Squatty Body"), his strong but occasionally erratic throwing arm (a quick sidearm release sometimes sailed a ball into center field), and especially about any glimpses of tenderness beneath that barbed wire exterior. One writer who called Munson "a closet nice guy" was told to "go to hell." But not without, the writer noted, a trace of smile.

By 1976 Munson was an established star, a five-time All-Star, and that year the American League's Most Valuable Player. Then, at career's peak, he received a couple of jolts. The first came from Cincinnati manager Sparky Anderson. In a clubhouse interview after the Reds had swept the Yankees in the 1976 World Series (in which Munson had batted a searing .529 and finished the Series with a record-tying six straight hits), Anderson was asked to compare Munson with his own Johnny Bench, the universally acknowledged emperor of all catchers. Flush with world championship elation, Sparky opined that it would be "embarrassing" to compare anybody to Johnny Bench. The widely disseminated quote made Thurman's Ohio winter a bit colder. Then, in the spring of 1977, he received a worse jolt.

● *Reggie Jackson, the straw that stirred things up.*

The Yankees had signed free agent Reggie Jackson, a man whose talent was exceeded only by his sparkling self-image. Reggie had already said he wasn't coming to New York to be a star, that he was bringing his star to the big city. Also, Jackson's contract was more dollar-laden than Munson's, after club owner George Steinbrenner had assured his catcher of being the team's highest-paid player.

And then there appeared in *Sport Magazine* a Reggie story in which the self-confidently outspoken Jackson—who, remember, was joining a team of pennant winners—was quoted as saying, "You know, this team . . . it all flows from me. I've got to keep it all going. I'm the straw that stirs the drink. . . . Munson thinks he can be the straw that stirs the drink, but he can only stir it bad."

● *Yankee manager Billy Martin.*

Word of Reggie's ill-phrased pomposity spread quickly through the Yankee clubhouse. Team captain and league MVP Munson brooded over the story (while sportswriters couldn't resist writing about "the straw that broke the catcher's back").

"I don't think Thurm ever got over it," one teammate said. "I think it bothered him for the rest of his life." (Once, after hitting a home run, Munson crossed home plate and ignored the congratulatory hand extended by Reggie.)

Munson bulled his way through the 1977 season, playing 149 games despite an infected hand, leg spasms, headaches, and a seriously banged-up knee. He delivered a .308 season and one hundred RBIs and helped the Yankees to another pennant and this time a world championship (and probably took sullen satisfaction when he pulled more MVP votes than Jackson).

After the 1977 season, Munson asked Steinbrenner to arrange a trade with Cleveland so Thurman could spend more time with his wife and three children (teammates said that his devotion to his family was exceptional). But, according to one Yankee front office executive, Steinbrenner felt that "Thurman was indispensable and irreplaceable, and wasn't going to trade him." There was, in fact, no catcher in the league, with the exception of Boston's Carlton Fisk, who was a match for Munson's talents. And even if he could get statistical parity for him, Steinbrenner knew that no other catcher could bring Munson's leadership and other intangibles to the Yankees.

In Munson's last full season, 1978, the Yankees won a third successive pennant and for the second year in a row upended the Los Angeles Dodgers in the World Series, helped by Munson's seven RBIs in six games. This was typical of the hitting he did in post-season competition, when the pressure was greatest. In three pennant playoff series, the Yankee catcher, whose reputation as a "money" hitter was surpassed by no one in the game, batted .339, and in three World Series, .373.

After having caught over one hundred games for nine straight seasons, Munson was beginning to pay the usual catcher's toll of painfully protesting legs, and going into the 1979 season there was increasing talk of easing his burden while keeping his lethal bat active as a designated hitter. But the aches and pains notwithstanding, Munson, with his defensive skills and his acute knowledge of the league's hitters, was still invaluable behind the plate, and he spent eighty-eight of his first ninety-seven games in 1979 holding up the big glove.

Munson was batting .288 after those ninety-seven games when the team had its off day on August 2, the day he decided to stop off at home, spend time with his family, and work out behind the controls of his Cessna Citation.

"They were a team of stars," one writer said of the Yankees. "But when Thurman died, they were like a team without a heart."

● *Munson has just missed Oakland's Angel Mangual, according to umpire Larry Barnett.*

● *Thurman Munson. "He was ready for anything back there," said Billy Martin.*

Ray Boone.

BOB
BOONE

When he was a boy, Bob Boone didn't think there was anything special about big league ballplayers. After all, they were frequent guests at the Boone home, and sometimes the boy would be taken to their place of business where he would sit in the clubhouse or even go out on the field and be allowed to toss a baseball back and forth with one of the players.

"I was about a year or so old when my father reached the big leagues," Bob said, "and since he played for a dozen years I grew up right in the middle of life in the big leagues. I took it all for granted, never realizing how lucky I was."

Bob's father Ray came up with Cleveland in 1948 and later played for Detroit, the Chicago White Sox, Kansas City Athletics, Milwaukee Braves, and Boston Red Sox, dividing his time between shortstop (his original position) and then third base and first base. Ray Boone could hit hard—he was the American League RBI co-leader in 1955 and hit twenty or more home runs in a season four times. It was the kind of career that keeps a family in pride for generations, but for this family, it was just the beginning.

Bob Boone was born in San Diego, on November 19, 1947. The young man grew to good size—6'2", just over 200 solidly hewn together pounds, with those good athletic genes helping to set it all in motion.

"My father never pushed us," Bob said ("us" meant he and his brother Rodney, who played minor league ball for four years). "But when he saw desire and ability, he was very encouraging and most helpful."

Bob didn't enter pro ball until 1969, when he was twenty-one years old, waiting until he had received a B.A. degree in psychology from Stanford University (an excellent field of study for a man who was to go on for nearly two decades working with pitchers, the acknowledged prima donnas of baseball).

The man who would one day establish the major league record for games caught was originally signed by the Philadelphia Phillies as a third baseman, a position he covered during his first two seasons in

Bob Boone with the Phillies in 1973.

"Of all the great catchers, and believe me he's one of them," a veteran National League scout said of Boone, "I think Boone is the one least appreciated by the general public because his contributions to winning games are so inconspicuous and subtle." Referring to the Phillies teams that won division titles in 1976, 1977, and 1978, the scout said, "Those weren't particularly great teams, outside of Mike Schmidt, Greg Luzinski, and Larry Bowa. And, except for Steve Carlton, the pitching wasn't so outstanding. So you looked behind the plate and saw what Boone was doing. You watched a ball game pitch by pitch and you saw him getting everything it was possible to get from a pitcher."

Paul Richards, himself a former catcher said of Boone, "I'll tell you where he absolutely excels: at blocking pitches in the dirt and keeping them in front of him. It isn't the prettiest play in baseball, but it's one of the most important defensive efforts a player can make, especially with a man on third. Boone does it as well as anybody I've ever seen. You don't often see Bob Boone chasing a ball back to the backstop. A blocked pitch can keep a man from scoring or from getting into scoring position, and it can keep a double play in order. It helps win more games than most people think, and when the game is over the only people who really know about it are the pitcher and manager."

With Johnny Bench, Gary Carter, and the hard-hitting (but defensively weak) Ted Simmons in the league, Boone was overshadowed. The Phillies catcher never hit with the authority of the others, although in Philadelphia's division-winning seasons he batted .271, .284, and .283, enhancing those averages with his skills at bunting and hitting-and-running. California Angels manager Gene Mauch has described Boone as baseball's most adept bunter, which is another illustration of Boone's quiet way of winning ball games.

In 1980 the Phillies won the division again and this time the pennant and World Series. Boone batted .412 in the Series, after a season

the minors. By 1972, he had been converted to catcher, with Eugene, Oregon, in the Pacific Coast League. At the end of the season he joined the Phillies, beginning the career that would carry him into the record books.

In 1973 Boone caught 145 games, a year later 146; by the end of the 1989 season he had caught over one hundred games in a season fifteen times, breaking the record of thirteen that had been jointly held by Bill Dickey and Johnny Bench.

Boone was neither flashy nor spectacular, he did not hit a lot of home runs (twelve being his tops for a single season).

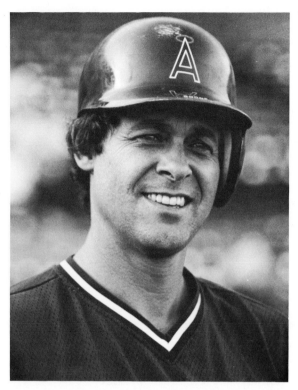

● *California Angels catcher Bob Boone, "The best quarterback in baseball," according to manager Gene Mauch.*

during which he had dipped to .229. When he slipped even further in the strike season of 1981, to .211, the Phillies felt the shadows were beginning to settle over him and sold him to the California Angels for a reported $300,000. (Those large cash transactions, once so common in baseball, hardly ever happen anymore.)

When Angels manager Gene Mauch heard that Boone was available, he told the club not to hesitate.

"Boone's the best quarterback in baseball," Mauch said.

His new catcher more than vindicated the skipper's appraisal; in Boone's first year in California, the Angels won the division title.

"It was impressive," a California writer said of the new catcher's performance. "Remember, he was taking over a staff he didn't know and working on hitters he didn't know. But it didn't take long before he knew what he had to know and the pitchers soon had absolute confidence in him. And he did what he had done in Philly— take a so-so staff and make a winner of it."

"The most important thing," Boone said, "is to stay with the pitcher's strength, not the batter's weakness." Another important thing was to strive to give his pitchers the confidence they needed. On one occasion, Angels ace righthander Mike Witt was seeing his changeups turning into line drives.

"Bob never said a word to me about the changeups," Witt said. "He knew I might have taken it the wrong way in the middle of a game. He just started calling fastballs and curves." Commenting on his catcher's uncanny way of synchronizing with a pitcher's thoughts, Witt said, "I guess that's why he was a psychology major at Stanford."

Boone's consummate skill at "converting" balls into strikes is given admiring attention in the enjoyably insightful book *The Diamond Appraised*, by Craig R. Wright, one of the top analysts of baseball statistics, and Tom House, a former major league pitcher and then pitching coach of the Texas Rangers (as well as the holder of a Ph.D. in Humanistic Studies from San Diego's University). After describing Boone as "probably the best example" of a catcher who "can motivate and direct a pitcher without the pitcher even knowing it's happening," the book goes on further about Boone:

> He's been an incredibly effective catcher for the Angels, even though it's obvious his physical tools aren't what they were a few years ago. One of Booney's tricks that's gotten a lot of attention is this business of "framing" the strike zone. That's kind of a

misnomer; what Boone does is actually *extend* the strike zone, and by up to six or eight inches. He'll set up in the corner, but with the heel of his glove in the strike zone. Then, when the pitcher throws the ball into the center of the glove—or sometimes even the webbing—it looks to the umpire as if it's still a strike. So he's added the whole width of the glove to the strike zone; you'd better believe that's a big edge for the pitcher.

Granted free agency after the 1988 season, Boone, now forty-one years old, signed with the Kansas City Royals and gave his new club a fine season, getting into 131 games and batting .274. By now the quiet veteran with the strong arm (a six-time leader in assists), sly mind, and durable body had moved into the pantheon of baseball's all-time catchers. No man of mask and mitt had ever caught more big league games, at the end of the 1989 season a total of 2,185.

"He's making it awfully hard," one writer said of the still-active Boone, "for anyone who wants to break that record."

● *Boone with Kansas City in 1989. Baseball's all-time leader in games caught.*

. . .

Gary Carter.

GARY CARTER

"**S**ometimes you couldn't believe it was the same guy," one opponent said. "Meet him off the field or around the batting cage and he was always this smiling, friendly guy. But then during the game, try scoring on a close play and it's like running into the side of a wall. I tell you, he can be *mean* at home plate."

The subject under discussion was Gary Carter, who at 6'2" and 210 cemented together pounds had the ideal build for a man whose job it was to defend the home plate portals against the charge of onrushing runners. By the end of the 1989 season, he had survived the injuries and the bruising collisions and the grinding wear and tear and rung up a total of 1,823 games caught, just thirty-eight fewer than the record for National League catchers set by Al Lopez.

Along with his durability and superb qualities as a defensive catcher (highlighted by a strong arm, a scrambling ruggedness in digging balls out of the dirt, and a reputation for astute pitch-calling), Carter swung one of the most potent bats of any catcher in history, hitting twenty or more home runs in a season nine times, driving in a hundred or more runs in a season four times, and

in 1984 tying for the RBI lead with 106, making him one of only three catchers ever to lead in runs batted in (Roy Campanella and Johnny Bench were the others).

Carter was born in Culver City, California, on April 8, 1954, and raised in nearby Fullerton. He was a star athlete at Sunnyhills High School (an aptly named school for a boy with his sparkling disposition), a bonfire at baseball, football, and basketball—he captained each team—as well as a good student, being elected to the National Honor Society. A nice boy to have in the neighborhood.

His athletic versatility was good enough to attract over one hundred college scholarship offers; but when the Montreal Expos selected him in the third round of the June 1972 free-agent draft, the eighteen-year-old headed into professional baseball to begin a career that would eventually be stamped with Hall of Fame credentials.

Three years of minor league polish and he was ready

for the glitter of penthouse baseball, joining the Expos in 1975, but not yet as the club's regular catcher. That job belonged to Barry Foote. Carter caught sixty-six games in 1975 and played the rest of the time in the outfield, batting .270 and hitting seventeen home runs (he made the All-Star team that year as an outfielder). In 1976 Foote bogged down to a .194 average—a statistical equivalent of body odor—and by 1977 Montreal's regular catcher was Gary Carter, Foote having been given, so to speak, the boot.

In his first full year behind the plate, the twenty-three-year-old Carter achieved instant stardom, catching 146 games, hitting thirty-one home runs, batting .284, and leading catchers with 101 assists. His only problem was not of his making—he was in the same league as the man who some were saying might be the greatest catcher of all time, Johnny Bench.

"It wasn't fair to Gary," one writer said, "but that's the way it goes. Bench was already a legend when Gary came up, and the truth was Johnny was beginning to slip just a bit, but there was no way you were going to say that *anybody* was better than Johnny Bench."

Carter, however, quickly carved out his own solid reputation and it wasn't long before no other catcher in baseball cast as long a shadow. He was behind the plate for the National League in every All-Star Game from 1979 through 1988 (with the exception of the 1985 game, which he missed because of injury).

Not long after he reached the majors Carter began attracting as much attention with his exuberance and bright keyboard of a smile as with his playing. Some of his teammates thought the zestful Carter personality a bit too bubbly and resented it.

Larry Parrish, who played in the minors and then at Montreal with Carter, said, "He smiled an awful lot, especially with cameras around. I didn't like him for years." But with the passage of time Parrish realized that Gary was "a competitor," and that the relentless enthusiasm was "real" and a genuine asset for a club.

● *Carter (right) with Montreal Expos teammate Pete Rose in 1984.*

Nevertheless, Carter's demonstrative personality continued to rankle. The higher his star rose in Montreal—and there was nobody more acclaimed on the Expos—the more attention he received. And he reveled in it. When he came to New York to play for the Mets in 1985, he helped infect the club with his emotional overdrive, egged on by the New York crowd that demanded "curtain calls" after home runs. Most players were shy about acknowledging the crowd, coming to the top step of the dugout and allowing a brief wave; but not Carter, who came out firing a clenched fist. The ardor wasn't popular with opposing teams. Carter's rationale for it had an ingenuous quality. He was, he said, "a very energetic person," one who loved playing and loved winning. It was as if his natural energy and enthusiasm combined with the joy of winning to produce a chemical reaction too powerful to contain.

● *A catcher's job can be hazardous, especially when 230-pound Dave Parker is intent on scoring.*

It wasn't easy to "really *know*" Carter, an Expo teammate said. "The kidding with him is a little stiff, forced. He's real image-conscious. He *acts* like Gary Carter."

"Gary always wanted to be liked by the team," Parrish said, "because everyone always liked him when he was growing up. His life was like the high school prom." Maybe, but not entirely, for Carter's ingratiating smile, which everyone seemed to think was perpetual, was a partial cover for the pain that never goes away—the death of his mother to leukemia when he was just twelve years old, an engulfing tragedy that Carter said he "took very personally, very hard."

Carter's popularity in Montreal became enormous. He moved his family to the city, took Berlitz courses in French, delighted in his nickname, "The Kid" (it derived from the boyish good cheer he brought with him to his first big league camp in 1975, when he bounded about like a

veritable Andy Hardy in spiked shoes). But this was one tough and durable kid; from 1977 through 1985 (excluding the strike-shortened 1981 season) he averaged 146 games a year behind the plate, with his occasional "days off" finding him at first base.

In 1979, Montreal lost the National League East title by two games to Pittsburgh. In 1980, Montreal again lost a close race, this time by one game to Philadelphia. In 1981, the Expos won in the east but lost a heartbreaking playoff series to the Los Angeles Dodgers on a pinch-hit home run in the ninth inning of the final game by Rick Monday.

The three successive near-miss disappointments left a sour taste in Montreal. Soon after, Carter was given a seven-year, $13.1 million contract, a pact that Montreal's top ownership began questioning in public, wondering if the star was worth it. After that, Carter would pick up a newspaper and find himself being undermined in anonymous quotes attributed to teammates. The gist was, Carter shouldn't be smiling so much and be so cheerful when the team was not winning pennants. A convoluted logic soon took shape in Montreal: Carter's faultless public image made him unpopular with his teammates and therefore he was hurting the team; and though he was easily the best player on the team, the Expos had never won a pennant with him.

The grumblings from north of the border were carefully noted by New York Mets general manager Frank Cashen, one of baseball's brightest minds and canniest operators. Realizing that players of Carter's stature are seldom traded, Cashen mentioned to Montreal GM John McHale that if the catcher ever became available the Mets would be interested. This conversation occurred in October 1983, during a Mets-Expos game in New York. More than a year later, on December 10, 1984, after a week of remarkably secret negotiations, the trade was made. In exchange for infielder Hubie Brooks, outfielder Herm Winningham, pitcher Floyd Youmans, and catcher Mike Fitzgerald, Gary Carter became a Met.

● *Gary Carter with the New York Mets in 1985.*

● *The New York Mets have just beaten the Boston Red Sox in the 1986 World Series, and Carter (right) is joining the celebration.*

In New York, Carter found a team poised for the spring to success. Enthusiastic fans were thronging to Shea Stadium in record numbers, giving thunderous vocal support to their heroes, and in this noisily upbeat and optimistic atmosphere Carter's effervescent personality was a perfect blend. He was also the perfect man to handle the sizzling young talent on the club's pitching staff that included Dwight Gooden, Ron Darling, Sid Fernandez, and, later, David Cone.

Carter wasted no time in endearing himself to Mets fans, his tenth-inning home run, giving the New Yorkers an Opening Day victory over the Cardinals. The new man gave his new club one of his finest all-around seasons, catching 143 games, hitting a career-high thirty-two home runs, driving in one hundred runs, and batting .281. Carter was a galvanizing factor in the club's ninety-eight victories and season-long contention for Eastern Division honors, which they lost in the season's waning days to the Cardinals by three games.

A year later, a rampaging Mets team won 108 regular-season games, won the division by a thundering twenty-one-and-a-half games and plunged into two of the most memorable post-season series in history, with several Carter hits figuring crucially in a world championship.

Though limited by injuries to 122 games behind the plate, his lowest total since 1976 (excepting the strike season), Carter hit twenty-four home runs and tied a team record with 105 RBIs. But then, in the pennant playoffs against Houston, the Mets star catcher suddenly found himself in a suffocating batting slump. Coming to bat in the twelfth inning of Game 5, he was a wretched 1 for 21. The series was tied at two games apiece and the score was balanced at 1–1, the Mets had a runner on second with one out. Carter picked

● *Carter is about to send that ball for a ride. The action took place in the eighth inning of the fourth game of the 1986 World Series. Carter sent the ball out for his second home run of the game. The pitcher is Steve Crawford, the catcher Rich Gedman, the umpire Joe Brinkman.*

this ripe moment to dissolve his slump with a game-winning rap through the middle and into center field.

In the World Series against the Boston Red Sox, Carter's two home runs in Game 4 helped the Mets deadlock the Series. And then in Game 6, with the Mets down 5–3 with two out in the bottom of the tenth, it was Carter's two-out single that began the rally that ended with Bill Buckner's famous error and enabled the Mets to tie the Series, which they won in Game 7.

In 1983, Carter had begun voicing fears of "burnout," the occupational fear of catchers who work nearly all of their team's games year after year. Citing Johnny Bench, whose aching body forced him to stop catching at the age of thirty-three, Carter said, "I don't want to cripple myself. I don't want to be just hanging on at thirty-five." Not yet thirty when he said this, he said that there were already times when "it takes me a half-hour to get out of bed. There are days when I can't walk down the stairs without stretching and popping my legs back into shape."

For Gary Carter the burnout began in 1987 and accelerated over the next two years. Although catching full seasons in 1987 and 1988, his offensive production began to diminish. In 1988 he contributed eleven home runs and forty-six RBIs to the Mets' division title.

In 1989, Carter suffered severely from that complaint common to catchers, retaliation from long-abused knees (his had by now undergone four operations). In a season of pain and frustration, Carter got into just fifty games, batting .183, with two home runs and fifteen RBIs. It was not a good time to have a contract run out. With regrets—and they were genuine, for Carter had helped lift the franchise to spectacular success—the Mets on November 14 released him.

Players of Gary Carter's stature, however, are not easily retired. An aura pervades even at twilight, and so on January 19, 1990, the man who in his time had been the best catcher in baseball, signed a conditional contract with the San Francisco Giants. When asked by reporters how he felt about playing for the Giants, Carter answered, ''Enthusiastic.'' As ever.

● *Gary Carter in 1989.*

AND NOT FORGETTING...

A list such as the one that forms this book is most interesting when severely limited, when it has been broken off at a point that virtually compels debate about who has been omitted. Following are brief summaries of some of the catchers whose exclusion from the list in this book can be legitimately questioned; competing lists of baseball's greatest catchers would undoubtedly include many of them. Since the scope of this book does not reach into the nineteenth century, the name of the most admired catcher of that distant baseball time, Charles (Buck) Ewing, is missing. Although Ewing, who played for five teams from 1880 to 1897, was a catcher for less than half of his 1,315 big league games, he was considered without equal in nineteenth century players at that position, a judgment that was certified by his remarkably early (1939) election to the Hall of Fame.

Al Lopez

Al Lopez was so highly regarded by the Brooklyn Dodgers that in 1931 the team traded Ernie Lombardi and kept Lopez. While he never hit as resoundingly as Lombardi, Lopez developed into one of the most skillful of all catchers (while compiling a modest but not negligible .261 lifetime average). Al played in the National League from 1928, 1930 through 1946, for Brooklyn, Boston, and Pittsburgh, catching a league record 1,861 games. He finished his playing career with Cleveland in 1947. He was later a pennant-winning manager with Cleveland and the Chicago White Sox, and was voted into the Hall of Fame in 1977.

Rick Ferrell

A Hall of Fame inductee in 1984, Rick Ferrell caught in the American League for St. Louis, Boston, and Washington, from 1929 through 1945 and 1947. He caught over one hundred games in a season ten times, and from 1931 through 1936 batted .290 or better. Lifetime average: .281.

Bill Freehan

Detroit's Bill Freehan (1961, 1963–1976) set a major league record for catchers by leading in fielding six straight years (1965–1970). Big and tough, he caught over one hundred games in a season ten times. His .993 fielding average is highest in history for catchers with 1,000 or more games. He hit two hundred lifetime home runs while compiling a .262 average.

Ted Simmons

Defensive liabilities kept Ted Simmons from making the front list in this book. One of baseball's greatest hitting catchers, he was a seven-time .300 hitter, with a .332 peak in 1975, eight times driving in over ninety runs in a season. He played for the St. Louis Cardinals, Milwaukee Brewers, and Atlanta Braves, from 1968 through 1988.

Walker Cooper

The hard-hitting Walker Cooper played for six National League clubs, from 1940 through 1957, hitting .300 six times and .285 lifetime. In 1947 he hit thirty-five home runs while playing for the New York Giants, one of the highest totals ever for a catcher. Cooper caught one hundred games in a season only five times.

Sherman Lollar

An eighteen-year American Leaguer (1946–1963) with Cleveland, New York, St. Louis, and then his last twelve years with the Chicago White Sox, Lollar was a steady hitter (.264) and a solid catcher who was strong in leadership qualities.

Lance Parrish

One of the heaviest-hitting of all catchers, Lance Parrish came up with Detroit in 1977, free-agented himself to Philadelphia in 1987, and was traded to California after the 1988 season. Through 1989 he had hit 261 home runs.

And . . .

Despite light stickwork, some catchers have enjoyed long and successful careers through sheer defensive brilliance. Among the most prominent of them are:

Jim Hegan, who played from 1941 through 1942 and 1946 through 1960, primarily for Cleveland, was considered without peer as an all-around defensive catcher (a .228 lifetime lends weight to this claim).

Jim Sundberg's catching credentials are impeccable. He played from 1974 through 1989, with Texas, Milwaukee, Kansas City, and the Chicago Cubs, catching 1,958 games. He led American League catchers in fielding seven times, with his .995 percentage in 1979 the highest in league history for a catcher with 150 games. He was a lifetime .248 hitter.

"If he and I were on the same team, I'd have to play third base." The speaker was Johnny Bench, the man he was referring to was Jerry Grote, who played from 1963 through 1964, 1966 through 1978, and 1981, mostly with the New York Mets. Grote's catching skills helped nurture such gifted young Mets pitchers as Tom Seaver, Jerry Koosman, Tug McGraw, and Nolan Ryan. He was a .252 career hitter.

LIFETIME RECORDS

Statistics reprinted by permission of *The Sporting News.*

Roger Bresnahan

Year Club	League	Pos.	G.	AB.	R.	H.	2B.	3B.	HR.	SB.	B.A.	PO.	A.	E.	F.A.
1897—Washington	Nat.	P	7	18	2	6	0	0	0	0	.333	2	8	0	1.000
1898—Toledo	Int.-State	P	4	12	0	5	3	0	0	0	.417	1	3	1	.800
1899—Minneapolis	West.	P-C	3	1	0	1	0	1	0	0	1.000	1	5	1	.857
1900—Chicago	Nat.	C	1	2	0	0	0	0	0	0	.000	0	0	0	.000
1901—Baltimore	Amer.	P-C	86	293	40	77	9	9	1	10	.263	193	69	20	.929
1902—Baltimore	Amer.	C-3-O	66	234	31	64	9	6	4	11	.274	141	72	20	.914
1902—New York	Nat.	C-INF	50	178	16	52	13	3	1	6	.292	113	25	8	.945
1903—New York	Nat.	OF	111	406	87	142	30	8	4	34	.350	150	14	6	.965
1904—New York	Nat.	OF	107	402	81	114	21	8	5	13	.284	151	14	8	.954
1905—New York	Nat.	C	95	331	58	100	18	3	0	11	.302	492	114	19	.970
1906—New York	Nat.	C-OF	124	405	69	114	22	4	0	25	.281	478	131	17	.973
1907—New York	Nat.	C	104	328	57	83	9	7	4	15	.253	483	97	8	.986
1908—New York	Nat.	C	139	449	70	127	25	3	1	14	.283	657	140	12	.985
1909—St. Louis	Nat.	C	69	234	27	57	4	1	0	11	.244	211	78	12	.960
1910—St. Louis	Nat.	C	78	234	35	65	15	3	0	13	.278	295	100	16	.961
1911—St. Louis	Nat.	C	78	227	22	63	17	8	3	4	.278	325	102	14	.968
1912—St. Louis	Nat.	C	48	108	8	36	7	2	1	4	.333	138	49	5	.974
1913—Chicago	Nat.	C	69	162	20	37	5	2	1	7	.228	194	67	10	.963
1914—Chicago	Nat.	C	101	248	42	69	10	4	0	14	.278	365	113	11	.978
1915—Chicago	Nat.	C	77	221	19	45	8	1	1	19	.204	345	95	8	.982
1916—Toledo	A. A.	C	44	120	19	29	6	1	2	4	.242	95	13	0	1.000
1917—Toledo	A. A.	C	40	80	10	22	5	0	0	1	.275	67	20	3	.967
1918—Toledo	A. A.	C	19	52	4	12	2	0	1	0	.231	24	1	1	.962
National League Totals			1258	3953	613	1110	204	57	21	190	.281	4399	1144	154	.973
American League Totals			152	527	71	141	18	15	5	21	.268	334	141	40	.922
Major League Totals			1410	4480	684	1251	222	72	26	211	.279	4733	1285	194	.969

Pitching Record

Year Club	League	G.	W.	L.	Pct.	SO.	BB.	H.
1897—Washington	National	7	4	0	1.000	12	8	52
1898—Toledo	Inter-State	4	2	2	.500	11	8	40
1899—Minneapolis	Western	3	0	2	.000	5	8	—
1901—Baltimore	American	1	0	0	.000	4	0	10
1910—St. Louis	National	1	0	0	.000	0	1	6
American League Totals		1	0	0	.000	4	0	10
National League Totals		8	4	0	1.000	12	8	58
Major League Totals		9	4	0	1.000	16	8	68

World Series Record

Year Club	League	Pos.	G.	AB.	R.	H.	2B.	3B.	HR.	SB.	B.A.	PO.	A.	E.	F.A.
1905-New York	Nat.	C	5	16	3	5	2	0	0	1	.313	27	7	0	1.000

Johnny Kling

Year Club	League	Pos.	G.	AB.	R.	H.	2B.	3B.	HR.	SB.	B.A.	PO.	A.	E.	F.A.
1896—Houston	Texas	OF-SS	51	—	47	—	7	5	3	18	.359	—	—	—	.879
1900—St. Joseph	West.	C	108	442	75	133	—	—	—	23	.303	441	107	28	.951
1900—Chicago	Nat.	C	15	51	8	15	3	1	0	0	.294	48	12	5	.923
1901—Chicago	Nat.	C-OF-1B	70	253	25	67	5	3	0	7	.266	398	70	20	.959
1902—Chicago	Nat.	C-SS	113	434	50	124	15	6	0	23	.286	477	160	15	.977
1903—Chicago	Nat.	C	132	491	67	146	29	13	3	23	.297	565	189	24	.969
1904—Chicago	Nat.	C-OF-1B	120	452	41	110	18	0	2	7	.243	499	135	17	.974
1905—Chicago	Nat.	C-OF-1B	110	380	26	83	8	6	1	13	.218	538	136	24	.966
1906—Chicago	Nat.	C-OF	99	343	45	107	15	8	2	14	.312	520	126	12	.982
1907—Chicago	Nat.	C-1B	100	334	44	95	15	8	1	9	.284	499	109	8	.987
1908—Chicago	Nat.	C-OF-1B	125	424	51	117	23	5	4	16	.276	596	149	16	.979
1909—															
1910—Chicago	Nat.	C	86	297	31	80	17	2	2	3	.269	407	118	11	.979
1911—Chicago-Boston	Nat.	C-3B	97	321	40	68	11	3	3	1	.212	424	140	26	.956
1912—Boston	Nat.	C	81	252	26	80	10	3	2	3	.317	322	108	19	.958
1913—Cincinnati	Nat.	C	80	209	20	57	7	6	0	2	.273	259	94	9	.975
Major League Totals—13 Years			1228	4241	474	1149	176	64	20	121	.271	5492	1546	206	.972

World Series Record

Year Club	League	Pos.	G.	AB.	R.	H.	2B.	3B.	HR.	SB.	B.A.	PO.	A.	E.	F.A.
1906—Chicago	Nat.	C	6	17	2	3	1	0	0	0	.176	37	10	1	.979
1907—Chicago	Nat.	C	5	19	2	4	0	0	0	0	.211	25	9	1	.971
1908—Chicago	Nat.	C	5	16	2	4	1	0	0	0	.250	32	6	0	1.000
1910—Chicago	Nat.	C	5	13	0	1	0	0	0	0	.077	11	7	0	1.000
World Series Totals—4 years			21	65	6	12	2	0	0	0	.185	105	32	2	.986

Ray Schalk

Year Club	League	Pos.	G.	AB.	R.	H.	2B.	3B.	HR.	RBI.	B.A.	PO.	A.	E.	F.A.
1911—Taylorville	Ill.-Mo.	C	47	161	27	64	—	—	—	—	.398	—	—	—	—
1911—Milwaukee	A. A.	C	31	76	9	18	2	1	0	—	.237	112	36	2	.987
1912—Milwaukee	A. A.	C	80	266	19	72	8	4	3	—	.271	354	108	7	.985
1912—Chicago	Amer.	C	23	63	7	18	2	0	0	6	.286	115	40	14	.917
1913—Chicago	Amer.	C	128	401	38	98	15	5	1	42	.244	586	153	15	.980
1914—Chicago	Amer.	C	135	392	30	106	13	2	0	37	.270	613	183	21	.974
1915—Chicago	Amer.	C	135	413	46	110	14	4	1	48	.266	655	159	13	.984
1916—Chicago	Amer.	C	129	410	36	95	12	9	0	36	.232	653	166	10	.988
1917—Chicago	Amer.	C	140	424	48	96	12	4	3	53	.226	624	148	15	.981
1918—Chicago	Amer.	C	108	333	35	73	6	3	0	24	.219	422	114	12	.978
1919—Chicago	Amer.	C	131	394	57	111	9	3	0	40	.282	551	130	13	.981
1920—Chicago	Amer.	C	151	485	64	131	25	5	1	61	.270	581	138	10	.986
1921—Chicago	Amer.	C	128	416	32	105	24	4	0	47	.252	453	129	9	.985
1922—Chicago	Amer.	C	142	442	57	124	22	3	4	60	.281	591	150	8	.989
1923—Chicago	Amer.	C	123	382	42	87	12	2	1	44	.228	481	93	10	.983
1924—Chicago	Amer.	C	57	153	15	30	4	2	1	11	.196	176	55	10	.959
1925—Chicago	Amer.	C	125	343	44	94	18	1	0	52	.274	368	99	8	.983
1926—Chicago	Amer.	C	82	226	26	60	9	1	0	32	.265	251	45	7	.977
1927—Chicago	Amer.	C	16	26	2	6	2	0	0	2	.231	24	8	0	1.000
1928—Chicago	Amer.	C	2	1	0	1	0	0	0	1	1.000	4	0	0	1.000
1929—New York	Nat.	C	5	2	0	0	0	0	0	0	.000	7	0	0	1.000
1930—Buffalo	Int.	C	1	3	1	2	0	0	0	0	.667	6	0	0	1.000
American League Totals			1755	5304	579	1345	199	48	12	596	.254	7148	1810	175	.981
National League Totals			5	2	0	0	0	0	0	0	.000	7	0	0	1.000
Major League Totals			1760	5306	579	1345	199	48	12	596	.253	7155	1810	175	.981

World Series Record

Year Club	League	Pos.	G	AB.	R.	H.	2B.	3B.	HR.	RBI.	B.A.	PO.	A.	E.	F.A.
1917—Chicago	Amer.	C	6	19	1	5	0	0	0	0	.263	32	5	2	.949
1919—Chicago	Amer.	C	8	23	1	7	0	0	0	2	.304	29	15	1	.978
World Series Totals			14	42	2	12	0	0	0	2	.286	61	20	3	.964

Gabby Hartnett

Year Club	League	Pos.	G.	AB.	R.	H.	2B.	3B.	HR.	RBI.	B.A.	PO.	A.	E.	F.A.
1921—Worcester	East.	C	100	345	38	91	21	7	3	—	.264	447	104	19	.967
1922—Chicago	Nat.	C	31	72	4	14	1	1	0	4	.194	79	29	2	.982
1923—Chicago	Nat.	C-1B	85	231	28	62	12	2	8	39	.268	413	39	5	.989
1924—Chicago	Nat.	C	111	354	56	106	17	7	16	67	.299	369	97	18	.963
1925—Chicago	Nat.	C	117	398	61	115	28	3	24	67	.289	409	114	23	.958
1926—Chicago	Nat.	C	93	284	35	78	25	3	8	41	.275	307	86	9	.978
1927—Chicago	Nat.	C	127	449	56	132	32	5	10	80	.294	479	99	16	.973
1928—Chicago	Nat.	C	120	388	61	117	26	9	14	57	.302	455	103	6	.989
1929—Chicago	Nat.	PH-C	25	22	2	6	2	1	1	9	.273	4	0	0	1.000
1930—Chicago	Nat.	C	141	508	84	172	31	3	37	122	.339	646	68	8	.989
1931—Chicago	Nat.	C	116	380	53	107	32	1	8	70	.282	444	68	10	.981
1932—Chicago	Nat.	C	121	406	52	110	25	3	12	52	.271	484	75	10	.982
1933—Chicago	Nat.	C	140	490	55	135	21	4	16	88	.276	550	77	7	.989
1934—Chicago	Nat.	C	130	438	58	131	21	1	22	90	.299	605	86	3	.996
1935—Chicago	Nat.	C	116	413	67	142	32	6	13	91	.344	477	77	9	.984
1936—Chicago	Nat.	C	121	424	49	130	25	6	7	64	.307	504	75	5	.991
1937—Chicago	Nat.	C	110	356	47	126	21	6	12	82	.354	436	65	2	.996
1938—Chicago	Nat.	C	88	299	40	82	19	1	10	59	.274	358	40	2	.995
1939—Chicago	Nat.	C	97	306	36	85	18	2	12	59	.278	336	47	3	.992
1940—Chicago	Nat.	C	37	64	3	17	3	0	1	12	.266	69	9	4	.951
1941—New York	Nat.	C	64	150	20	45	5	0	5	26	.300	138	15	1	.994
1942—Indianapolis	A. A.	C	72	186	17	41	12	2	4	24	.220	190	36	7	.970
1943—Jersey City	Int.	C	16	16	0	4	1	0	0	5	.250	9	4	1	.929
1944—Jersey City	Int.	C	31	11	1	2	1	0	0	6	.182	0	0	0	.000
Major League Totals			1990	6432	867	1912	396	64	236	1179	.297	7562	1269	143	.984

World Series Record

Year Club	League	Pos.	G.	AB.	R.	H.	2B.	3B.	HR.	RBI.	B.A.	PO.	A.	E.	F.A.
1929—Chicago	Nat.	PH	3	3	0	0	0	0	0	0	.000	0	0	0	.000
1932—Chicago	Nat.	C	4	16	2	5	2	0	1	1	.313	31	5	1	.973
1935—Chicago	Nat.	C	6	24	1	7	0	0	1	2	.292	33	6	0	1.000
1938—Chicago	Nat.	C	3	11	0	1	0	1	0	0	.091	14	3	0	1.000
World Series Totals			16	54	3	13	2	1	2	3	.241	78	14	1	.989

Mickey Cochrane

Year Club	League	Pos.	G.	AB.	R.	H.	2B.	3B.	HR.	RBI.	B.A.	PO.	A.	E.	F.A.
1923—Dover	East. Sh.	C	65	245	56	79	12	6	5	—	.322	222	70	13	.957
1924—Portland	P. C.	C	99	300	43	100	8	5	7	56	.333	278	49	14	.959
1925—Philadelphia	Amer.	C	134	420	69	139	21	5	6	55	.331	419	79	8	.984
1926—Philadelphia	Amer.	C	120	370	50	101	8	9	8	47	.273	502	90	15	.975
1927—Philadelphia	Amer.	C	126	432	80	146	20	6	12	80	.338	559	85	9	.986
1928—Philadelphia	Amer.	C	131	468	92	137	26	12	10	57	.293	645	71	25	.966
1929—Philadelphia	Amer.	C	135	514	113	170	37	8	7	95	.331	659	77	13	.983
1930—Philadelphia	Amer.	C	130	487	110	174	42	5	10	85	.357	654	69	5	.993
1931—Philadelphia	Amer.	C	122	459	87	160	31	6	17	89	.349	560	63	9	.986
1932—Philadelphia	Amer.	C	139	518	118	152	35	4	23	112	.293	652	94	5	.993
1933—Philadelphia	Amer.	C	130	429	104	138	30	4	15	60	.322	476	67	6	.989
1934—Philadelphia	Amer.	C	129	437	74	140	32	1	2	76	.320	517	69	7	.988
1935—Detroit	Amer.	C	115	411	93	131	33	3	5	47	.319	504	50	6	.989
1936—Detroit	Amer.	C	44	126	24	34	8	0	2	17	.270	159	13	3	.983
1937—Detroit	Amer.	C	27	98	27	30	10	1	2	12	.306	103	13	0	1.000
Major League Totals			1482	5169	1041	1652	333	64	119	832	.320	6409	840	111	.985

World Series Record

Year Club League	Pos.	G	AB.	R.	H.	2B.	3B.	HR.	RBI.	B.A.	PO.	A.	E.	F.A.
1929—Philadelphia .... Amer.	C	5	15	5	6	1	0	0	0	.400	59	2	0	1.000
1930—Philadelphia .... Amer.	C	6	18	5	4	1	0	2	4	.222	39	1	1	.976
1931—Philadelphia .... Amer.	C	7	25	2	4	0	0	0	1	.160	40	4	1	.978
1934—Detroit .... Amer.	C	7	28	2	6	1	0	0	1	.214	36	5	0	1.000
1935—Detroit .... Amer.	C	6	24	3	7	1	0	0	1	.292	32	3	1	.972
World Series Totals		31	110	17	27	4	0	2	7	.245	206	15	3	.987

Bill Dickey

Year Club League	Pos.	G.	AB.	R.	H.	2B.	3B.	HR.	RBI.	B.A.	PO.	A.	E.	F.A.
1925—Little Rock .... South.	C	3	10	1	3	0	0	0	—	.300	8	2	0	1.000
1926—Muskogee .... W.A.	C	61	212	27	60	6	2	7	—	.283	300	58	13	.965
1926—Little Rock .... South.	C	21	46	6	18	1	5	0	8	.391	36	4	2	.952
1927—Jackson .... Cot. St.	C	101	364	46	108	31	3	3	—	.297	457	84	9	.984
1928—Little Rock .... South.	C	60	203	22	61	12	6	4	32	.300	151	52	8	.962
1928—Buffalo .... Int.	C	3	8	0	1	0	1	0	0	.125	12	4	2	.889
1928—New York .... Amer.	C	10	15	1	3	1	1	0	2	.200	6	2	0	1.000
1929—New York .... Amer.	C	130	447	60	145	30	6	10	65	.324	476	95	12	.979
1930—New York .... Amer.	C	109	366	55	124	25	7	5	65	.339	418	51	11	.977
1931—New York .... Amer.	C	130	477	65	156	17	10	6	78	.327	670	78	3	.996
1932—New York .... Amer.	C	108	423	66	131	20	4	15	84	.310	639	53	9	.987
1933—New York .... Amer.	C	130	478	58	152	24	8	14	97	.318	721	82	6	.993
1934—New York .... Amer.	C	104	395	56	127	24	4	12	72	.322	527	49	8	.986
1935—New York .... Amer.	C	120	448	54	125	26	6	14	81	.279	536	62	3	.995
1936—New York .... Amer.	C	112	423	99	153	26	8	22	107	.362	499	61	14	.976
1937—New York .... Amer.	C	140	530	87	176	35	2	29	133	.332	692	80	7	.991
1938—New York .... Amer.	C	132	454	84	142	27	4	27	115	.313	518	74	8	.987
1939—New York .... Amer.	C	128	480	98	145	23	3	24	105	.302	571	57	7	.989
1940—New York .... Amer.	C	106	372	45	92	11	1	9	54	.247	425	55	3	.994
1941—New York .... Amer.	C	109	348	35	99	15	5	7	71	.284	422	45	3	.994
1942—New York .... Amer.	C	82	268	28	79	13	1	2	37	.295	322	44	9	.976
1943—New York .... Amer.	C	85	242	29	85	18	2	4	33	.351	322	37	2	.994
1944-45—New York ...... Amer.	C					(in military service)								
1946—New York .... Amer.	C	54	134	10	35	8	0	2	10	.261	201	29	3	.987
1947—Little Rock .... South.	C	8	12	2	4	2	0	1	2	.333	13	2	0	1.000
Major League Totals		1789	6300	930	1969	343	72	202	1209	.313	7965	954	108	.988

World Series Record

Year Club League	Pos.	G	AB.	R.	H.	2B.	3B.	HR.	RBI.	B.A.	PO.	A.	E.	F.A.
1932—New York .... Amer.	C	4	16	2	7	0	0	0	4	.438	25	1	0	1.000
1936—New York .... Amer.	C	6	25	5	3	0	0	1	5	.120	38	4	1	.977
1937—New York .... Amer.	C	5	19	3	4	0	1	0	3	.211	26	1	0	1.000
1938—New York .... Amer.	C	4	15	2	6	0	0	1	2	.400	31	5	0	1.000
1939—New York .... Amer.	C	4	15	2	4	0	0	2	5	.267	27	2	0	1.000
1941—New York .... Amer.	C	5	18	3	3	1	0	0	1	.167	24	2	0	1.000
1942—New York .... Amer.	C	5	19	1	5	0	0	0	0	.263	25	1	1	.963
1943—New York .... Amer.	C	5	18	1	5	0	0	1	4	.278	28	3	0	1.000
World Series Totals		38	145	19	37	1	1	5	24	.255	224	19	2	.992

Ernie Lombardi

Year Club	League	Pos.	G.	AB.	R.	H.	2B.	3B.	HR.	RBI.	B.A.	PO.	A.	E.	F.A.
1926—Oakland	P.C.	C	4	6	2	2	1	0	0	—	.333	8	0	0	1.000
1927—Oakland	P.C.	C	16	20	2	3	0	0	1	6	.150	12	4	0	1.000
1927—Ogden	Utah-Idaho	C	50	186	29	74	16	1	4	—	.398	183	40	9	.961
1928—Oakland	P.C.	C	120	318	39	120	27	3	8	47	.377	257	47	15	.953
1929—Oakland	P.C.	C	164	516	70	189	36	3	24	109	.366	521	95	16	.975
1930—Oakland	P.C.	C	146	473	76	175	32	4	22	105	.370	563	105	17	.975
1931—Brooklyn	Nat.	C	73	182	20	54	7	1	4	23	.297	218	23	4	.984
1932—Cincinnati	Nat.	C	118	413	43	125	22	9	11	68	.303	288	76	14	.963
1933—Cincinnati	Nat.	C	107	350	30	99	21	1	4	47	.283	223	52	8	.972
1934—Cincinnati	Nat.	C	132	417	42	127	19	4	9	62	.305	383	61	5	.989
1935—Cincinnati	Nat.	C	120	332	36	114	23	3	12	64	.343	298	49	6	.983
1936—Cincinnati	Nat.	C	121	387	42	129	23	2	12	68	.333	330	54	15	.962
1937—Cincinnati	Nat.	C	120	368	41	123	22	1	9	59	.334	333	58	11	.973
1938—Cincinnati	Nat.	C	129	489	60	167	30	1	19	95	.342	512	73	9	.985
1939—Cincinnati	Nat.	C	130	450	43	129	26	2	20	85	.287	536	63	10	.984
1940—Cincinnati	Nat.	C	109	376	50	120	22	0	14	74	.319	397	46	5	.989
1941—Cincinnati	Nat.	C	117	398	33	105	12	1	10	60	.264	496	70	10	.983
1942—Boston	Nat.	C	105	309	32	102	14	0	11	46	.330	251	41	6	.980
1943—New York	Nat.	C	104	295	19	90	7	0	10	51	.305	296	36	10	.971
1944—New York	Nat.	C	117	373	37	95	13	0	10	58	.255	350	47	13	.968
1945—New York	Nat.	C	115	368	46	113	7	1	19	70	.307	425	49	8	.983
1946—New York	Nat.	C	88	238	19	69	4	1	12	39	.290	272	36	7	.978
1947—New York	Nat.	C	48	110	8	31	5	0	4	21	.282	86	11	2	.980
1948—Sacra.-Oak	P.C.	C	102	284	25	75	13	0	11	55	.264	267	37	8	.974
Major League Totals			1853	5855	601	1792	277	27	190	990	.306	5694	845	143	.979

World Series Record

Year Club	League	Pos.	G	AB.	R.	H.	2B.	3B.	HR.	RBI.	B.A.	PO.	A.	E.	F.A.
1939—Cincinnati	Nat.	C	4	14	0	3	0	0	0	2	.214	22	1	1	.958
1940—Cincinnati	Nat.	C-PH	2	3	0	1	1	0	0	0	.333	4	0	0	1.000
World Series Totals			6	17	0	4	1	0	0	2	.235	26	1	1	.964

Yogi Berra

Year Club	League	Pos.	G.	AB.	R.	H.	2B.	3B.	HR.	RBI.	B.A.	PO.	A.	E.	F.A.
1943—Norfolk	Pied.	C	111	376	52	95	17	8	7	56	.253	480	75	16	.972
1944–45—Kansas City ...	A. A.						(in military service)								
1946—Newark	Int.	C-OF	77	277	41	87	14	1	15	59	.314	344	45	11	.973
1946—New York	Amer.	C	7	22	3	8	1	0	2	4	.364	28	6	0	1.000
1947—New York	Amer.	C-OF	83	293	41	82	15	3	11	54	.280	307	18	9	.973
1948—New York	Amer.	C-OF	125	469	70	143	24	10	14	98	.305	390	40	9	.979
1949—New York	Amer.	C	116	415	59	115	20	2	20	91	.277	544	60	7	.989
1950—New York	Amer.	C	151	597	116	192	30	6	28	124	.322	777	64	13	.985
1951—New York	Amer.	C	141	547	92	161	19	4	27	88	.294	693	82	13	.984
1952—New York	Amer.	C	142	534	97	146	17	1	30	98	.273	700	73	6	.992
1953—New York	Amer.	C	137	503	80	149	23	5	27	108	.296	566	64	9	.986
1954—New York	Amer.	C-3B	151	584	88	179	28	6	22	125	.307	718	64	8	.990
1955—New York	Amer.	C	147	541	84	147	20	3	27	108	.272	721	54	13	.984
1956—New York	Amer.	C-OF	140	521	93	155	29	2	30	105	.298	733	57	11	.986
1957—New York	Amer.	C-OF	134	482	74	121	14	2	24	82	.251	707	61	4	.995
1958—New York	Amer.	C-OF-1B	122	433	60	115	17	3	22	90	.266	558	44	2	.997
1959—New York	Amer.	C-OF	131	472	64	134	25	1	19	69	.284	706	62	4	.995
1960—New York	Amer.	C-OF	120	359	46	99	14	1	15	62	.276	312	24	5	.985
1961—New York	Amer.	OF-C	119	395	62	107	11	0	22	61	.271	237	15	2	.992
1962—New York	Amer.	C-OF	86	232	25	52	8	0	10	35	.224	238	17	6	.977
1963—New York	Amer.	C	64	147	20	43	6	0	8	28	.293	244	13	3	.988
1964—New York	Amer.						(Did not play—served as manager.)								
1965—New York	Nat.	C	4	9	1	2	0	0	0	0	.222	15	1	1	.941
American League Totals			2116	7546	1174	2148	321	49	358	1430	.285	9179	818	124	.988
National League Totals			4	9	1	2	0	0	0	0	.222	15	1	1	.941
Major League Totals			2120	7555	1175	2150	321	49	358	1430	.285	9194	819	125	.988

Released by New York Yankees, October 16, 1964.

World Series Record

Year—Club	League	Pos.	G	AB.	R.	H.	2B.	3B.	HR.	RBI.	B.A.	PO.	A.	E.	F.A.
1947—New York	Amer.	C-OF	6	19	2	3	0	0	1	2	.158	21	2	2	.920
1949—New York	Amer.	C	4	16	2	1	0	0	0	1	.063	37	3	0	1.000
1950—New York	Amer.	C	4	15	2	3	0	0	1	2	.200	30	1	0	1.000
1951—New York	Amer.	C	6	23	4	6	1	0	0	0	.261	27	3	1	.968
1952—New York	Amer.	C	7	28	2	6	1	0	2	3	.214	59	7	1	.985
1953—New York	Amer.	C	6	21	3	9	1	0	1	4	.429	36	3	0	1.000
1955—New York	Amer.	C	7	24	5	10	1	0	1	2	.417	40	4	0	1.000
1956—New York	Amer.	C	7	25	5	9	2	0	3	10	.360	50	3	0	1.000
1957—New York	Amer.	C	7	25	5	8	1	0	1	2	.320	44	2	1	.979
1958—New York	Amer.	C	7	27	3	6	3	0	0	2	.222	60	6	0	1.000
1960—New York	Amer.	C-OF-PH	7	22	6	7	0	0	1	8	.318	18	1	0	1.000
1961—New York	Amer.	OF	4	11	2	3	0	0	1	3	.273	11	0	1	.917
1962—New York	Amer.	C	2	2	0	0	0	0	0	0	.000	6	1	0	1.000
1963—New York	Amer.	PH	1	1	0	0	0	0	0	0	.000	0	0	0	.000
World Series Totals			75	259	41	71	10	0	12	39	.274	439	36	6	.988

Roy Campanella

Year—Club	League	Pos.	G.	AB.	R.	H.	2B.	3B.	HR.	RBI.	B.A.	PO.	A.	E.	F.A.
1946—Nashua	New Eng.	C	113	396	75	115	19	8	13	96	.290	687	64	15	.980
1947—Montreal	Int.	C	135	440	64	120	25	3	13	75	.273	642	83	9	.988
1948—St. Paul	A.A.	C-OF	35	123	31	40	5	2	13	39	.325	147	19	6	.965
1948—Brooklyn	Nat.	C	83	279	32	72	11	3	9	45	.258	413	45	9	.981
1949—Brooklyn	Nat.	C	130	436	65	125	22	2	22	82	.287	684	55	11	.985
1950—Brooklyn	Nat.	C	126	437	70	123	19	3	31	89	.281	683	54	11	.985
1951—Brooklyn	Nat.	C	143	505	90	164	33	1	33	108	.325	722	72	11	.986
1952—Brooklyn	Nat.	C	128	468	73	126	18	1	22	97	.269	662	55	4	.994
1953—Brooklyn	Nat.	C	144	519	103	162	26	3	41	142	.312	807	57	10	.989
1954—Brooklyn	Nat.	C	111	397	43	82	14	3	19	51	.207	600	58	7	.989
1955—Brooklyn	Nat.	C	123	446	81	142	20	1	32	107	.318	672	54	6	.992
1956—Brooklyn	Nat.	C	124	388	39	85	6	1	20	73	.219	659	49	11	.985
1957—Brooklyn	Nat.	C	103	330	31	80	9	0	13	62	.242	618	51	5	.993
Major League Totals			1215	4205	627	1161	178	18	242	856	.276	6520	550	85	.988

Incurred injuries in automobile accident, January 28, 1958, which ended his playing career.

World Series Record

Year—Club	League	Pos.	G	AB.	R.	H.	2B.	3B.	HR.	RBI.	B.A.	PO.	A.	E.	F.A.
1949—Brooklyn	Nat.	C	5	15	2	4	1	0	1	2	.267	32	2	0	1.000
1952—Brooklyn	Nat.	C	7	28	0	6	0	0	0	1	.214	39	5	0	1.000
1953—Brooklyn	Nat.	C	6	22	6	6	0	0	1	2	.273	47	9	0	1.000
1955—Brooklyn	Nat.	C	7	27	4	7	3	0	2	4	.259	42	3	1	.978
1956—Brooklyn	Nat.	C	7	22	2	4	1	0	0	3	.182	49	3	0	1.000
World Series Totals			32	114	14	27	5	0	4	12	.237	209	22	1	.996

Johnny Bench

Year—Club	League	Pos.	G.	AB.	R.	H.	2B.	3B.	HR.	RBI.	B.A.	PO.	A.	E.	F.A.
1965—Tampa	Fla. St.	C-OF	68	214	29	53	13	1	2	35	.248	415	40	6	.987
1966—Peninsula	Carol.	C	98	350	59	103	16	0	22	68	.294	692	87	17	.979
1966—Buffalo	Int.	C	1	0	0	0	0	0	0	0	.000	2	0	0	1.000
1967—Buffalo	Int.	C-3-O-1	98	344	39	89	17	2	23	68	.259	577	82	13	.981
1967—Cincinnati	Nat.	C	26	86	7	14	3	1	1	6	.163	175	16	1	.995
1968—Cincinnati	Nat.	C	154	564	67	155	40	2	15	82	.275	942	102	9	.991
1969—Cincinnati	Nat.	C	148	532	83	156	23	1	26	90	.293	793	76	7	.992
1970—Cincinnati	Nat.	C-O-1-3	158	605	97	177	35	4	45	148	.293	854	78	15	.984
1971—Cincinnati	Nat.	C-O-1-3	149	562	80	134	19	2	27	61	.238	735	67	10	.988
1972—Cincinnati	Nat.	C-O-1-3	147	538	87	145	22	2	40	125	.270	791	63	10	.988

Year	Club	League	Pos.	G.	AB.	R.	H.	2B.	3B.	HR.	RBI.	B.A.	PO.	A.	E.	F.A.
1973—Cincinnati	Nat.	C-O-1-3	152	557	83	141	17	3	25	104	.253	757	63	6	.993
1974—Cincinnati	Nat.	C-3B-1B	160	621	108	174	38	2	33	129	.280	794	123	9	.990
1975—Cincinnati	Nat.	C-OF-1B	142	530	83	150	39	1	28	110	.283	646	52	8	.989
1976—Cincinnati	Nat.	C-OF-1B	135	465	62	109	24	1	16	74	.234	655	60	4	.994
1977—Cincinnati	Nat.	C-O-1-3	142	494	67	136	34	2	31	109	.275	735	69	11	.987
1978—Cincinnati	Nat.	C-1B-OF	120	393	52	102	17	1	23	73	.260	680	53	9	.988
1979—Cincinnati	Nat.	C-1B	130	464	73	128	19	0	22	80	.276	632	69	10	.986
1980—Cincinnati	Nat.	C	114	360	52	90	12	0	24	68	.250	505	39	5	.991
1981—Cincinnati	Nat.	1B-C	52	178	14	55	8	0	8	25	.309	375	28	7	.983
1982—Cincinnati	Nat.	3B-1B-C	119	399	44	103	16	0	13	38	.258	108	159	19	.934
1983—Cincinnati	Nat.	3-1-C-O	110	310	32	79	15	2	12	54	.255	292	74	10	.973
Major League Totals—17 Years			2158	7658	1091	2048	381	24	389	1376	.267	10469	1191	150	.987

Championship Series Record

Year	Club	League	Pos.	G	AB.	R.	H.	2B.	3B.	HR.	RBI.	B.A.	PO.	A.	E.	F.A.
1970—Cincinnati	Nat.	C	3	9	2	2	0	0	1	1	.222	20	3	0	1.000
1972—Cincinnati	Nat.	C	5	18	3	6	1	1	1	2	.333	28	3	1	.969
1973—Cincinnati	Nat.	C	5	19	1	5	2	0	1	1	.263	31	2	0	1.000
1975—Cincinnati	Nat.	C	3	13	1	1	0	0	0	0	.077	18	4	0	1.000
1976—Cincinnati	Nat.	C	3	12	3	4	1	0	1	1	.333	11	4	0	1.000
1979—Cincinnati	Nat.	C	3	12	1	3	0	1	1	1	.250	17	2	0	1.000
Championship Series Totals—6 Years			22	83	11	21	4	2	5	6	.253	125	18	1	.993

World Series Record

Year	Club	League	Pos.	G	AB.	R.	H.	2B.	3B.	HR.	RBI.	B.A.	PO.	A.	E.	F.A.
1970—Cincinnati	Nat.	C	5	19	3	4	0	0	1	3	.211	36	3	0	1.000
1972—Cincinnati	Nat.	C	7	23	4	6	1	0	1	1	.261	41	7	1	.980
1975—Cincinnati	Nat.	C	7	29	5	6	2	0	1	4	.207	44	6	0	1.000
1976—Cincinnati	Nat.	C	4	15	4	8	1	1	2	6	.533	18	2	0	1.000
World Series Totals—4 Years			23	86	16	24	4	1	5	14	.279	139	18	1	.994

Thurman Munson

Year	Club	League	Pos.	G.	AB.	R.	H.	2B.	3B.	HR.	RBI.	B.A.	PO.	A.	E.	F.A.
0000—Binghamton	East.	C	71	226	28	68	12	3	6	37	.301	327	53	9	.977
0000—Syracuse	Int.	C-2-3	28	102	13	37	9	1	2	17	.363	81	13	6	.940
0000—New York	Amer.	C	26	86	6	22	1	2	1	9	.256	119	18	2	.986
0000—New York	Amer.	C	132	453	59	137	25	4	6	53	.302	631	80	8	.989
1971—New York	Amer.	C-OF	125	451	71	113	15	4	10	42	.251	547	67	1	.998
1972—New York	Amer.	C	140	511	54	143	16	3	7	46	.280	575	71	15	.977
1973—New York	Amer.	C	147	519	80	156	29	4	20	74	.301	673	80	12	.984
1974—New York	Amer.	C	144	517	64	135	19	2	13	60	.261	743	75	22	.974
1975—New York	Amer.	C-1-O-3	157	597	83	190	24	3	12	102	.318	725	95	23	.973
1976—New York	Amer.	C-OF	152	616	79	186	27	1	17	105	.302	546	78	14	.978
1977—New York	Amer.	C	149	595	85	183	28	5	18	100	.308	657	73	12	.984
1978—New York	Amer.	C-OF	154	617	73	183	27	1	6	71	.297	698	61	11	.986
1979—New York	Amer.	C-1B	97	382	42	110	18	3	3	39	.288	428	44	10	.979
Major League Totals			1423	5344	696	1558	229	32	113	701	.292	6342	742	130	.982

Selected by New York Yankees' organization in 1st round (fourth player selected) of free-agent draft, June 7, 1968.

Championship Series Record

Year	Club	League	Pos.	G	AB.	R.	H.	2B.	3B.	HR.	RBI.	B.A.	PO.	A.	E.	F.A.
1976—New York	Amer.	C	5	23	3	10	2	0	0	3	.435	18	6	2	.923
1977—New York	Amer.	C	5	21	3	6	1	0	1	5	.286	24	4	0	1.000
1978—New York	Amer.	C	4	18	2	5	1	0	1	2	.278	22	4	0	1.000
Championship Series Totals			14	62	8	21	4	0	2	10	.339	64	14	2	.975

World Series Record

Year	Club	League	Pos.	G	AB.	R.	H.	2B.	3B.	HR.	RBI.	B.A.	PO.	A.	E.	F.A.
1976—New York	Amer.		C	4	17	2	9	0	0	0	2	.529	21	7	0	1.000
1977—New York	Amer.		C	6	25	4	8	2	0	1	3	.320	40	5	0	1.000
1978—New York	Amer.		C	6	25	5	8	3	0	0	7	.320	33	5	0	1.000
World Series Totals				16	67	11	25	5	0	1	12	.373	94	17	0	1.000

Carlton Fisk

Year	Club	League	Pos.	G.	AB.	R.	H.	2B.	3B.	HR.	RBI.	B.A.	PO.	A.	E.	F.A.
1967—Greenville	W. Car.							(in military service)								
1968—Waterloo	Midw.		C	62	195	31	66	11	2	12	34	.338	385	42	8	.982
1969—Pittsfield	East.		C	97	309	38	75	18	3	10	41	.243	551	65	22	.966
1969—Boston	Amer.		C	2	5	0	0	0	0	0	0	.000	2	0	0	1.000
1970—Pawtucket	East.		C-OF-1B	93	284	43	65	18	1	12	44	.229	482	50	7	.987
1971—Louisville	Int.		C-OF-3B	94	308	45	81	10	4	10	43	.263	588	51	13	.980
1971—Boston	Amer.		C	14	48	7	15	2	1	2	6	.313	72	6	2	.975
1972—Boston	Amer.		C	131	457	74	134	28	9	22	61	.293	846	72	15	.984
1973—Boston	Amer.		C	135	508	65	125	21	0	26	71	.246	739	50	14	.983
1974—Boston	Amer.		C	52	187	36	56	12	1	11	26	.299	267	26	6	.980
1975—Boston	Amer.		C	79	263	47	87	14	4	10	52	.331	347	30	8	.979
1976—Boston	Amer.		C	134	487	76	124	17	5	17	58	.255	649	73	12	.984
1977—Boston	Amer.		C	152	536	106	169	26	3	26	102	.315	779	69	11	.987
1978—Boston	Amer.		C-OF	157	571	94	162	39	5	20	88	.284	734	90	17	.980
1979—Boston	Amer.		C-OF	91	320	49	87	23	2	10	42	.272	155	8	3	.982
1980—Boston	Amer.		C-1-O-3	131	478	73	138	25	3	18	62	.289	543	56	11	.982
1981—Chicago	Amer.		C-1-3-O	96	338	44	89	12	0	7	45	.263	479	46	6	.989
1982—Chicago	Amer.		C-1B	135	476	66	127	17	3	14	65	.267	648	63	5	.993
1983—Chicago	Amer.		C	138	488	85	141	26	4	26	86	.289	709	46	7	.991
1984—Chicago	Amer.		C	102	359	54	83	20	1	21	43	.231	421	38	6	.987
1985—Chicago	Amer.		C	153	543	85	129	23	1	37	107	.238	801	60	10	.989
1986—Chicago	Amer.		C-OF	125	457	42	101	11	0	14	63	.221	455	44	8	.984
1987—Chicago	Amer.		C-1B-OF	135	454	68	116	22	1	23	71	.256	597	66	7	.990
1988—Chicago	Amer.		C	76	253	37	70	8	1	19	50	.277	338	36	2	.995
1989—Chicago	Amer.		C	103	375	47	110	25	2	13	68	.293	419	37	3	.993
Major League Totals—20 Years				2141	7603	1155	2063	371	46	336	1166	.271	10000	916	153	.993

Championship Series Record

Year	Club	League	Pos.	G	AB.	R.	H.	2B.	3B.	HR.	RBI.	B.A.	PO.	A.	E.	F.A.
1975—Boston	Amer.		C	3	12	4	5	1	0	0	2	.417	15	0	0	1.000
1983—Chicago	Amer.		C	4	17	0	3	1	0	0	0	.176	27	3	0	1.000
Championship Series Totals—2 Years				7	29	4	8	2	0	0	2	.276	42	3	0	1.000

World Series Record

Year	Club	League	Pos.	G	AB.	R.	H.	2B.	3B.	HR.	RBI.	B.A.	PO.	A.	E.	F.A.
1975—Boston	Amer.		C	7	25	5	6	0	0	2	4	.240	37	3	2	.952

Bob Boone

Year	Club	League	Pos.	G.	AB.	R.	H.	2B.	3B.	HR.	RBI.	B.A.	PO.	A.	E.	F.A.
1969—Raleigh-Durham ...	Carol.		3B	80	300	45	90	13	1	5	46	.300	71	160	20	.920
1970—Reading	East.		3B	20	80	12	23	2	0	2	10	.288	28	38	7	.904
1971—Reading	East.		3B-C-SS	92	328	41	87	14	3	4	37	.265	206	138	17	.953
1972—Eugene	P.C.		C	138	513	77	158	32	4	17	67	.308	699	77	24	.970
1972—Philadelphia	Nat.		C	16	51	4	14	1	0	1	4	.275	66	7	5	.936
1973—Philadelphia	Nat.		C	145	521	42	136	20	2	10	61	.261	868	89	10	.990
1974—Philadelphia	Nat.		C	146	488	41	118	24	3	3	52	.242	825	77	22	.976
1975—Philadelphia	Nat.		C-3B	97	289	28	71	14	2	2	20	.246	459	48	5	.990
1976—Philadelphia	Nat.		C-1B	121	361	40	98	18	2	4	54	.271	587	39	6	.990
1977—Philadelphia	Nat.		C-3B	132	440	55	125	26	4	11	66	.284	654	83	8	.989
1978—Philadelphia	Nat.		C-1B-OF	132	435	48	123	18	4	12	62	.283	650	55	8	.989
1979—Philadelphia	Nat.		C-3B	119	398	38	114	21	3	9	58	.286	527	66	8	.987
1980—Philadelphia	Nat.		C	141	480	34	110	23	1	9	55	.229	741	88	18	.979
1981—Philadelphia	Nat.		C	76	227	19	48	7	0	4	24	.211	365	32	6	.985
1982—California	Amer.		C	143	472	42	121	17	0	7	58	.256	650	87	8	.989
1983—California	Amer.		C	142	468	46	120	18	0	9	52	.256	606	83	14	.980
1984—California	Amer.		C	139	450	33	91	16	1	3	32	.202	660	71	12	.984
1985—California	Amer.		C	150	460	37	114	17	0	5	55	.248	670	71	10	.987
1986—California	Amer.		C	144	442	48	98	12	2	7	49	.222	812	84	11	.988
1987—Palm Springs	Calif.		C	3	9	0	1	1	0	0	0	.111	17	4	1	.955
1987—California	Amer.		C	128	389	42	94	18	0	3	33	.242	684	56	13	.983
1988—California	Amer.		C	122	352	38	104	17	0	5	39	.295	506	66	8	.986
1989—Kansas City	Amer.		C	131	405	33	111	13	2	1	43	.274	752	64	7	.991
National League Totals—10 Years				1125	3690	349	957	172	21	65	456	.259	5742	584	96	.958
American League Totals—8 Years				1099	3438	319	853	128	5	40	361	.248	5340	582	83	.986
Major League Totals—18 Years				2224	7128	668	1810	300	26	105	817	.254	11082	1166	179	.986

Division Series Record

Year	Club	League	Pos.	G	AB	R.	H.	2B.	3B.	HR.	RBI.	B.A.	PO.	A.	E.	F.A.
1981—Philadelphia	Nat.		C	3	5	0	0	0	0	0	0	.000	10	2	0	1.000

Championship Series Record

Year	Club	League	Pos.	G	AB	R.	H.	2B.	3B.	HR.	RBI.	B.A.	PO.	A.	E.	F.A.
1976—Philadelphia	Nat.		C	3	7	0	2	0	0	0	1	.286	8	2	0	1.000
1977—Philadelphia	Nat.		C	4	10	1	4	0	0	0	0	.400	18	2	0	1.000
1978—Philadelphia	Nat.		C	3	11	0	2	0	0	0	0	.182	16	2	1	.947
1980—Philadelphia	Nat.		C	5	18	1	4	0	0	0	2	.222	22	3	0	1.000
1982—California	Amer.		C	5	16	3	4	0	0	1	2	.250	30	3	0	1.000
1986—California	Amer.		C	7	22	4	10	0	0	1	2	.455	33	3	0	1.000
Championship Series Totals—6 Years				27	84	9	26	0	0	2	9	.310	127	15	1	.993

World Series Record

Year	Club	League	Pos.	G	AB	R.	H.	2B.	3B.	HR.	RBI.	B.A.	PO.	A.	E.	F.A.
1980-Philadelphia	Nat.		C	6	17	3	7	2	0	0	4	.412	49	3	0	1.000

Gary Carter

Year	Club	League	Pos.	G.	AB.	R.	H.	2B.	3B.	HR.	RBI.	B.A.	PO.	A.	E.	F.A.
1972—Cocoa Expos	Fla. E. C.	C-1B-3B	18	71	6	17	3	0	2	9	.239	111	12	10	.925
1972—W. Palm Beach	Fla. St.	C	20	50	9	16	2	2	0	5	.320	84	12	2	.980
1973—Quebec City	East.	C-1B-OF	130	439	65	111	16	1	15	68	.253	823	75	20	.978
1973—Peninsula	Int.	C	8	25	2	7	2	0	0	1	.280	5	1	0	1.000
1974—Memphis	Int.	C-1B-3B	135	441	62	118	14	7	23	83	.268	908	76	12	.988
1974—Montreal	Nat.	C-OF	9	27	5	11	0	1	1	6	.407	28	4	0	1.000
1975—Montreal	Nat.	OF-C-3B	144	503	58	136	20	1	17	68	.270	430	38	9	.981
1976—Montreal	Nat.	C-OF	91	311	31	68	8	1	6	38	.219	364	42	2	.995
1977—Montreal	Nat.	C-OF	154	522	86	148	29	2	31	84	.284	813	101	9	.990
1978—Montreal	Nat.	C-1B	157	533	76	136	27	1	20	72	.255	787	83	10	.989
1979—Montreal	Nat.	C	141	505	74	143	26	5	22	75	.283	751	88	9	.989
1980—Montreal	Nat.	C	154	549	76	145	25	5	29	101	.264	822	108	7	.993
1981—Montreal	Nat.	C-1B	100	374	48	94	20	2	16	68	.251	515	58	4	.993
1982—Montreal	Nat.	C	154	557	91	163	32	1	29	97	.293	954	104	10	.991
1983—Montreal	Nat.	C-1B	145	541	63	146	37	3	17	79	.270	855	108	5	.995
1984—Montreal	Nat.	C-1B	159	596	75	175	32	1	27	106	.294	990	78	7	.993
1985—New York	Nat.	C-1B-OF	149	555	83	156	17	1	32	100	.281	987	70	8	.992
1986—New York	Nat.	C-1-O-3	132	490	81	125	14	2	24	105	.255	943	70	9	.991
1987—New York	Nat.	C-1B-OF	139	523	55	123	18	2	20	83	.235	886	70	9	.991
1988—New York	Nat.	C-1B-3B	130	455	39	110	16	2	11	46	.242	842	58	10	.989
1989—New York	Nat.	C-1B	50	153	14	28	8	0	2	15	.183	266	31	6	.980
1989—Tidewater	Int.	C-1B	5	16	2	3	0	0	1	3	.188	26	1	1	.964
Major League Totals—16 Years				2008	7194	955	1907	329	30	304	1143	.265	11233	1111	114	.991

Division Series Record

Year	Club	League	Pos.	G	AB.	R.	H.	2B.	3B.	HR.	RBI.	B.A.	PO.	A.	E.	F.A.
1981—Montreal	Nat.	C	5	19	3	8	3	0	2	6	.421	21	5	0	1.000

Championship Series Record

Shares Championship Series records for most game-winning RBIs, total series (3) and series (2), 1986.

Year	Club	League	Pos.	G	AB.	R.	H.	2B.	3B.	HR.	RBI.	B.A.	PO.	A.	E.	F.A.
1981—Montreal	Nat.	C	5	16	3	7	1	0	0	0	.438	27	3	0	1.000
1986—New York	Nat.	C	6	27	1	4	1	0	0	2	.148	42	5	0	1.000
1988—New York	Nat.	C	7	27	0	6	1	1	0	4	.222	58	1	0	1.000
Championship Series Totals—3 Years				18	70	4	17	3	1	0	6	.243	127	9	0	1.000

World Series Record

Year	Club	League	Pos.	G	AB.	R.	H.	2B.	3B.	HR.	RBI.	B.A.	PO.	A.	E.	F.A.
1986—New York	Nat.	C	7	29	4	8	2	0	2	9	.276	57	1	0	1.000

INDEX

More Baseball Books to Order from
Wm. C. Brown's Line Up Are:

☐ **THE LAST .400 HITTER**
by John B. Holway

1991/304 pages/Cloth/ISBN 14129/$19.95

In the Summer of 1941 Ted Williams and Joe DiMaggio stood at the most dramatic peaks of their lives. DiMaggio created a legend in the best two months he ever played. Williams reached a height that no other man has scaled in 60 years. John B. Holway tells us the story about the famous last .400 hitter—Ted Williams.

☐ **THE GREATEST CATCHERS OF ALL TIME**
by Don Honig

1991/160 pages/Cloth/ISBN 12806/$18.95

A one-of-a-kind book—a one-of-a-kind series. In this unique book, Donald Honig highlights the careers of the 15 greatest catchers of all time.

☐ **THE PITTSBURGH CRAWFORDS: Memories of Black Baseball's Most Exciting Team**
by Jim Bankes

1991/195 pages/Paper/ISBN 12889/$15.95

A tribute to the most talented team in the National Negro League during the '30s: the Pittsburgh Crawfords.

☐ **BASEBALL BY THE BOOKS**
by Andy McCue

1990/175 pages/Paper/ISBN 12764/$14.95

If you love baseball and love reading about it even more, this book is a must for you! For over three years, Andy McCue has researched, gathered, and compiled over 1,300 entries in his new baseball fiction bibliography.

☐ **TEACHING THE MENTAL ASPECTS OF BASEBALL: A Coach's Handbook**
by Al Figone, Humboldt State University

1990/240 pages/Paper/ISBN 12767/$15.95

At last! A practical book for coaches and players of all levels about integrating the mental aspects of baseball when executing the technical skills.

☐ **BUILDING A BETTER HITTER**
by Stephen Pecci; Foreword by George Foster

1990/112 pages/Paper/ISBN 11404/$10.95

There's more to successful hitting than just good swings. Pecci's new book provides coaches and players with a program that produces better hitters.

☐ **THE COMPLETE BASEBALL HANDBOOK: Strategies and Techniques for Winning**
by Walter Alston and Don Weiskopf

1984/530 pages/Cloth/ISBN 6819/$19.95

Drawing upon 23 years of experience as manager of the Brooklyn/L.A. Dodgers—seven league pennants, and four World Series Championships—the late Walter Alston's time-honored philosophy on both the basics and fine points of coaching is geared toward producing better ball players and winning teams!

ORDER FORM

TO ORDER ANY OR ALL OF THESE TITLES:

1. **CALL Toll Free 1–800–338–5578**

2. Send check or money order plus appropriate state tax and $1.00 shipping and handling for each book ordered along with a list of the books you would like to receive (include ISBN numbers) to:

Wm. C. Brown Publishers
2460 Kerper Boulevard
Dubuque, Iowa 52001

SHIP TO: _____   Book Total $ _____

_____   Tax $ _____

City _____ State _____ Zip _____   Shipping $ _____

Total $ _____

REMEMBER TO ASK FOR A **FREE** SPORTS PAGE CATALOG LISTING ALL OF OUR TITLES